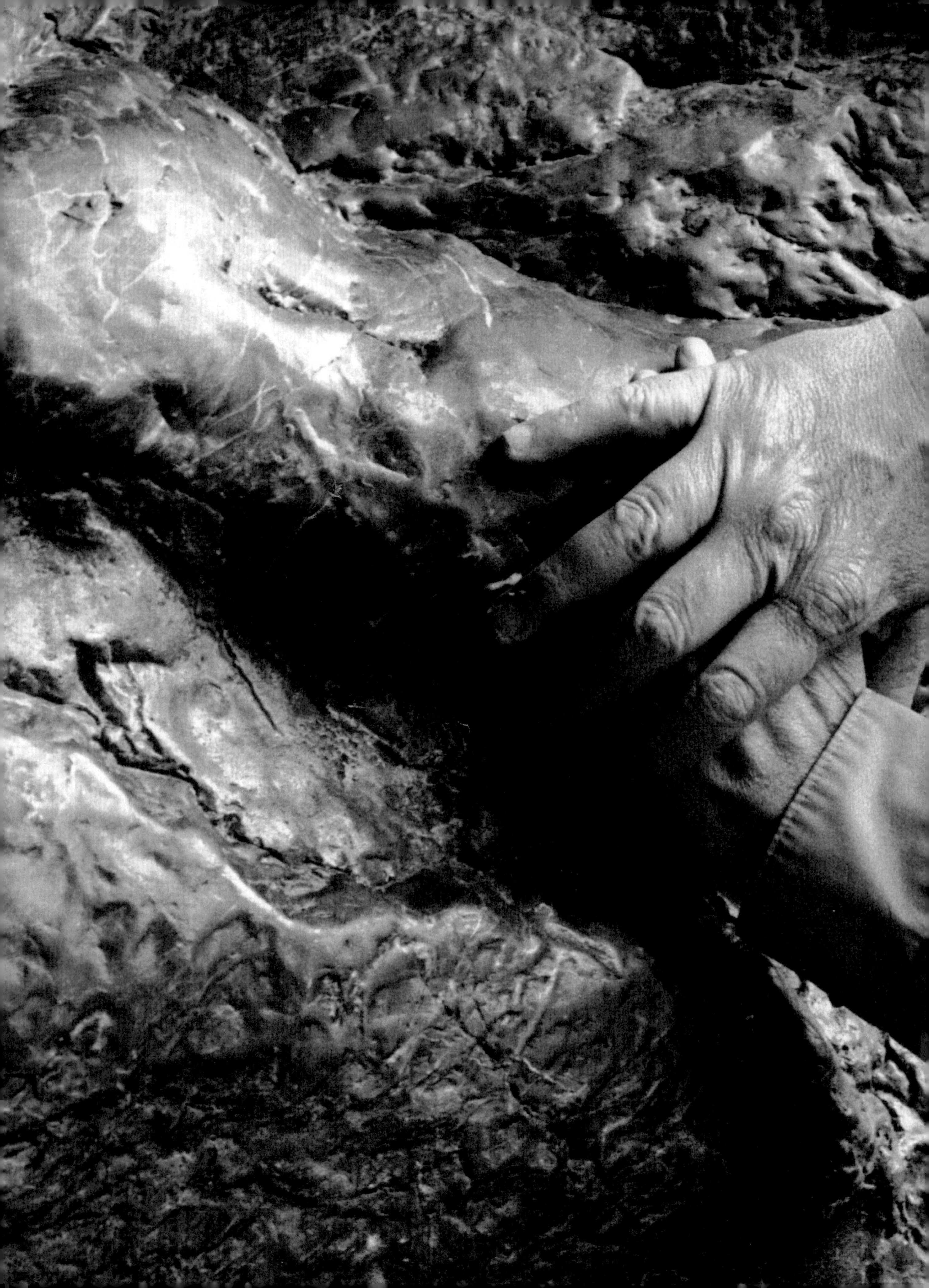

# Miracles

*The Presence of God in Our Lives*

**Cover:** In Medjugorje, Bosnia and Herzegovina; ART ZAMUR/GAMMA/GETTY. **Back cover:** The northern lights over Sweden; BABAK TAFRESHI/NATIONAL GEOGRAPHIC CREATIVE/GETTY. **Page 1:** In Lourdes, France, pilgrims pass their hands over the stone of the grotto; ABBAS/MAGNUM. **Pages 2–3:** First Communion in Oaxaca, Mexico; DAVID ALAN HARVEY/MAGNUM. **These pages:** A Pentecostal pilgrimage in Sumuleu, Romania; SZILARD KOSZTICSAK/MTI/AP.

# Table of Contents

RICHARD T. NOWITZ

## Introduction

# Let There Be Light

*There are among us secularists, scientists and seekers. There are wonderers and wanderers. There are skeptics and true believers. We are here and alive, and therefore have to ask: Might that be a miracle?*

ON THE OPPOSITE PAGE WE SEE AN olive tree at sunset in the Judaean Hills outside Bethlehem in Israel, near what is called Shepherds' Field. We all know that events transpired here. At the very least, a mother delivered a baby in a grotto just over two millennia ago. Perhaps unexpected visitors came to pay homage.

Were there miraculous events occurring that night, or simply ordinary happenings?

In this book we are accepting of miracles. We are accepting of loaves and fishes, and when we venture to Lourdes or Fátima, we do not do so with an inquisitor's attitude. On the opposite end of the spectrum, we don't have any pictures of statues weeping blood nor of baked goods resembling the Holy Virgin. You really can't produce a book on miracles and represent to the jury that you are entirely "clear-eyed." Miracles are not, by nature (and nature often vies with miracles), clear-eyed occurrences. However, we have tried to take a relatively clear-eyed approach. This world we live in is without a doubt wonderful, and therefore it might be a world that supports the wondrous—even the miraculous.

We will not prove here that Saint Joseph of Cupertino flew through the air all those centuries ago, but we will testify that Saint Katharine Drexel of Philadelphia was a saint to African Americans and Native Americans in need in our own time. Does a miracle have to have evidence of the supernatural, or can it just be miraculous? That is a question that is posed on almost every page of our book.

LIFE magazine was founded in 1936, during what Henry Luce called "the American Century." The 20th century was, often, a time of large, unexpected, even "miraculous" events. It has been fun, in putting together this volume, to revisit some of our reporting from back then. In '36, when assembling a staff for his imagined weekly periodical, which would show Americans "life" itself—"the world"—Luce hired four staff photographers. One of these was Alfred Eisenstaedt; Carl Mydans would become the fifth. Fine—even great—photo essays assembled by the two men are in these pages: Eisenstaedt, known to us as Eisie, visiting the famous pilgrimage site in Lourdes; Mydans traveling coast-to-coast in the postwar United States to put together one of the very first reports on the rise of Pentecostalism. More recently, LIFE sent the writer Tom Junod to Medjugorje to look at the miracles there. Those miracles have been a constant topic of ours, and this serves us well as we assemble these accounts.

We're not big fans of overlong and overanalytical "think pieces," but the large idea of miracles asks for some contemplation. On the next page, we begin with a preface that wrestles gently with this idea. And then we proceed through the modern and not-so-modern history of miracles. It is a trip we have enjoyed taking, and we hope you will enjoy joining us as we walk this path once more.

And now we walk on.

# Do You Believe in Miracles?

*That has been the question since the creation of Eden, and for many it remains the question today: Is this God's work I'm seeing?*

by Robert Sullivan

*Our wondrous universe: the Milky Way and Jupiter as seen from the Holy Land, where great and miraculous events transpired.*

BABAK TAFRESHI/SCIENCE SOURCE

PATRICK SICCOLI/GAMMA/GETTY

GOD MADE THE WORLD IN A WEEK. Later, He appeared to Moses, bequeathed the Ten Commandments and parted the Red Sea. Christ raised Lazarus from the dead and subsequently ascended to Heaven. Muhammad ascended as well. The Virgin appeared to children at Lourdes and then Fátima. In our time, it is said, she came again, and talked to two boys and four girls in Medjugorje, a jagged, high-country town of, at that moment in 1981, just about 1,000 souls (now, around 4,000) in what was then Yugoslavia and is today Bosnia and Herzegovina. Those youths, now grown, are still alive; they are sentient and consistent witnesses to something that much of the world believes was miraculous and that Rome has yet to deny. So let us start our examination of miracles with that phenomenon, and with what a miracle means to us all in the modern day and age. To some, it represents mysticism, perhaps. But multitudes accept that the extraordinary occurrence at Medjugorje (pronounced *MEHD-joo-gore-yeh*) was miraculous. Tens of millions have made pilgrimages there since 1981—from America and Australia, from Ireland and Italy, from Mexico and Spain, from the Philippines and France—and who is to say that any of them ventured in vain?

It happened late in June of '81. *Medjugorje* means "between the mountains," and one day two teenage girls were walking and talking on the path that leads to Mount Podbrdo, now known far and wide as "Apparition Hill." Medjugorje is a stunning place but hardly a pretty one; its peaks are gray, rough and slaggy. On that day, the girls were strolling in the craggy dreariness when, suddenly, in the distance, they perceived a woman with an ethereal glow emanating from her. She was not standing upon the ground but floating just above it. "*Gospa*," one girl exclaimed: "Our Lady." The girls hurried off, stunned.

They came back with some friends, and the vision appeared again, with a baby in her arms. The young people returned again and then again, and because they did, the six of them are known today as "the visionaries": Ivanka Ivankovic, 15 years old in 1981; Mirjana Dragicevic, 16; Ivan Dragicevic, 16 as well, but not Mirjana's twin (none of the visionaries is related); Vicka Ivankovic, 16, and destined to become the most famous of the group; Marija Pavlovic, 16; and Jakov Colo, only 10. On their first visit as a group, they approached the woman they were now sure was the Virgin and fell to their knees at her feet. They worshiped. Mother Mary spoke to them. She stressed that she wanted the young people to pray daily, to fast, to say the rosary and to find inner peace.

Similar visions had happened decades earlier, also with children. The famous appearances in Lourdes, France, and Fátima, Portugal—and we will visit those places, and those miracles, later in these pages—seem now as precursors to Medjugorje. But this, in Medjugorje, occurred in our own sophisticated age, and was bound to undergo harsh secular-humanist scrutiny. As Tom Junod wrote in LIFE of the six children precisely one decade after they had been chosen by the Virgin, "Since then they have been condemned and celebrated, prodded and poked, monitored by machines, interrogated by priests, police, psychologists, reporters and pilgrims. And yet ten years after their first walk up Apparition Hill, only one fact remains beyond dispute: Every evening, no matter where they are, whether in Medjugorje or in another country, the visionaries fall to their knees, gaze toward heaven and move their lips in mute appeal to an image no one else can see."

The Catholic Church, of course, has supported many miracles subsequent to those of Christ, including all the ones credited to its saints as well as the incidents at Fátima and Lourdes, and has left the door open for reverence of possible miracles behind such things as the Shroud of Turin. In the more than three decades since the apparitions in Medjugorje, the bishop of Mostar has refused to credit the events. However, in 2010 the Church of Rome announced that its Congregation for the Doctrine of the Faith would convene a commission of religious leaders, theologians and secular experts to look into the matter. And before his death in 2005, the beloved Pope John Paul II, perhaps the most Marian of pontiffs ever to sit upon Saint Peter's throne, spoke several times of his belief that something very special had happened at Medjugorje.

WHAT IS A MIRACLE? IS IT THE EXPERIENCE of a skydiver whose chute doesn't open but who bounces sideways down a hill and is left without a scratch? Is it the golden retriever who tugs a toddler out of harm's way as an SUV rounds the curve? Is it the walk-off home run on an oh-and-two breaking ball on the far outside corner?

Not for our purposes. This will be a book about miracles considered in a religious context. Now, these, too, run the gamut. People have sworn to figurines shedding tears of blood in backyard flower gardens, and of Mary's likeness reflected in shimmering plate-glass windows or truck stop pastries. And there has been everything in between. Patrick O'Boyle, who worked in the New York City borough of Queens, once told LIFE's David Van Biema: "What happened was last year we got into a recession. The houses weren't selling. So a couple of real estate people started buying Saint Joseph statues for their clients. That goes back 200 years to Europe. When nuns wanted a piece of land for their convents and such, they'd bury a religious medal on the property, and, lo and behold, the owner'd offer it to them. So people began to bury Saint Joseph statues, upside down, facing the house, and the house'd sell. Being a church goods salesman, I used to stock six at a time, but all of a sudden people were ordering 36, or 42, and we'd be dealing in cartons and cartons. We thought it was Christmas. They say, 'It's a miracle.' How you going to knock 'em for five-fifty each?"

O'Boyle's personal miracle, in terms of unanticipated sales, is different by degrees than those of his clients, but his testimony leads to a point worth making: This is not an Old Europe or Third World or New Age question, this question of miracles. It is global, and it is in our neck of the woods—as American as "In God We Trust."

***Where Mary first appeared to the children in Medjugorje, a cross was placed and immediately became the focus of pilgrimages.***

THE ART ARCHIVE/ART RESOURCE, NY

When we are young, we take faith on faith, which is to say, the miraculous and mysterious are just as acceptable as the Darwinian or Newtonian facts put in front of us by our teachers. As we grow older, the questions get more intricate and difficult to reconcile. Yet polls continue to show that the great majority of people in the United States—up to 80 percent—believe that miracles occur, and that these miracles have been engineered by God. The late priest Andrew Greeley, who wrote religious and sociological tracts as well as potboiler novels, put it this way, while never saying that he himself did *not* believe in miracles: "Americans are a wonder-hungry people."

We surely are. It is perhaps a product of our generally optimistic outlook. (Why not be hopeful and proud, when your democracy has succeeded better than any other ever invented?) It is certainly a part of our Judeo-Christian tradition, in which miracles have ever been at the heart of the story—the heart of the *history*—from, literally, Day One (of seven). God created the heavens and the earth. That surely was a miracle. God appeared to Adam and Eve: That was a miracle. Later, in the Bible, the burning bush was a sign, and of course a miracle. Later still, in the New Testament, water becoming wine and loaves that fed multitudes were miracles. The healing of the sick was one of Jesus's famous miracles, and the same act has been credited to other miracle workers in the many centuries since. When Pope John Paul II was canonized a saint in the spring of 2014, his posthumous intercession in healing in the temporal realm was noted as miraculous.

Certainly Native American worship was and is steeped in miracles: a god or the many gods influencing life on earth on a daily basis. Even the Puritans, who were as violently opposed to what they considered Rome's hocus-pocus as they were to the King of England's iron hand, brought to American shores a healthy belief in some forms of supernaturalism, including the miraculous evils of witches and warlocks, whom they notoriously persecuted in New England. Many of us consider all-American Quakers to be clear-thinking, sensible folk. Their founder, Englishman George Fox, made his reputation in the 17th century in part because it was said he could raise the dead. In the 18th century, so many of his next-generation adherents were attracted to European mystics that Jonathan Edwards was compelled to speak out against these miracle-spewing foreigners and "French prophets" in particular. Miracle workers are always attractive when day-to-day life is hard.

The Founding Fathers were, for the most part, deists; if they were affiliated with a specific religion, it was usually with what now comes under the general banner of Unitarianism. Theirs was a rationalist philosophy that respected God but felt His miracle-working was largely finished with the Creation, a thinking that thus accommodated, very comfortably, the separation of church and state and the concepts of "live and let live" and "the pursuit of happiness." We were free to pursue happiness on our own and not wait for a miracle to deliver something so precious yet ephemeral.

The United States, which seems today something of a miracle in and of itself, was formed as a pragmatic, decidedly non-miraculous nation. Our governmental, educational and cultural spheres had no place for miracles; in fact, they had much less space for any of the kind of romance that bulwarked similar institutional structures in Europe.

And here comes the big *Ah, but.*

Ah, but: While the structure of the nation was sound, solid, even stolid, the mind of the people was wild. It had been fueled by the success of the new enterprise. *We had pulled this off,* we were the new chosen people. As Van Biema wrote in LIFE: "The story of American religion is in part one of successive upheavals, as great numbers of American Christians deemed the dominant faiths of their periods too tame, too bureaucratized, too unconcerned with God's day-to-day involvement in human affairs. The result has been the mutation or invention of dozens of denominations—Methodism in the 1780s; Mormonism in the 1830s; certain Baptist groups before the Civil War; Pentecostalism in 1906; and, lately, the Charismatic movement—that are based on one miraculous event or teach that God makes miracles daily. Simultaneously, immigration brought in millions of devout Germans, Poles, Irish, Italians and Eastern European Jews with faith unpolluted by rationalist doubts." In other words: a happy and hopeful melting pot of, if not miracle seekers, miracle welcomers.

Kenneth L. Woodward was for decades the religion editor of *Newsweek* and wrote scores of cover stories for that magazine. He once piquantly explained for LIFE the push-pull of Miraculous America: "Let's suppose I'm working-class Boston. I read the *Globe*; I watch the news. That's the overculture, telling me what to think about, and probably ignoring the miraculous. But then after work I go to a local bar and talk to my friends, and that's the subculture, which determines my real attitude about what's been put on my plate. And an awful lot of these subcultures are accepting of, if not expectant of, miracles."

Woodward's Beantown reflection (which did not even consider all of the recent Patriots and Red Sox championships) is very much to the point: Do you believe in miracles? And if not, why not? Isn't the miraculous life richer?

This delivers us, especially while we are still dwelling on the United States, to all of the out-there miracles and apparitions. Today, what with Photoshop, no one believes in Jesus-in-the-clouds imagery anymore. But back in the day, when American fighter planes were heading into action over North Korea in the foreground of a famous photograph, and a distant, carefully sculpted (which is to say, doctored) cumulonimbus seemed quite like Christ bestowing his blessing, newspaper readers went: "Wow." So maybe we all doubt pictures now, but still: Christian-centric apparitions have been, in the technological age, reported in the sky over Lubbock, Texas; on a soybean storage tank in Fostoria, Ohio; on a refrigerator in Estill Springs, Tennessee; on a Pizza Hut billboard in Stone Mountain, Georgia; on the side of an office building in Clearwater, Florida; and on all those doughnuts and croissants and cheese sandwiches in roadhouses from Rome, Georgia, to Athens, Texas, to Paris, Tennessee. In New York City there are Hasidic Jews who will tell you that the

**Adam and Eve in the Garden,** ***a circa-1600 painting by Peter Paul Rubens at the Rubens House in Antwerp, Belgium.***

CORBIS

leavings from their rebbe's table might cure you, or get you married (finally!). Once upon a time, Protestantism, the Puritans notwithstanding, stood in opposition to Catholicism's magical thinking, but *today,* God-fearing televangelists will help you out of poverty, and maybe out of cancer.

Professor Robert Orsi, formerly of Harvard Divinity School and now teaching at Northwestern University, published *The Cambridge Companion to Religious Studies* and has looked into the social and cultural history of late-19th- and 20th-century Catholic childhoods in the United States. Asked about the tensions—and the attractions—of the miraculous to Americans, he told LIFE: "An anthropologist said that three things seem to demand that we direct at them a stream of symbols to make sense of them: physical pain, the experience of evil and the uncanny. Everybody has such experiences at one time or another. And if you were brought up in the Church, its symbols are available for use. Even a Catholic who considers himself a skeptic would, if he found his world being unmade by pain, death or evil, have recourse to the common vocabulary of the sacred, which includes miracles." Michael Fishbane, professor of Jewish Studies at the University of Chicago, took this thought to a different tradition for us as he imagined a secularized Jew walking along the Western Wall in Jerusalem and finding himself moved to push a petitioning prayer for a sick relation into one of the cracks: "And if you were to ask, even seconds later, 'Do you believe God will hear this prayer and heal so-and-so?' you might get a blank stare in response. But to take that stare at face value would be to miss a spontaneous moment of genuine belief."

Is it belief, or is it hope? Well, that's the question, isn't it—that, and how do hope and faith relate? We're terrified of God—we're God-*fearing*—and yet we love Him and want Him and often need Him. We want His help and inspiration, and we believe.

Many paragraphs ago we met Patrick O'Boyle of Queens, who as a businessman—a "Christian-goods salesman"—may have seemed somewhat cynical. He admitted to LIFE in the same conversation, "I'm not an over-religious man. I'm born and brought up a Catholic, I believe in my Church. But I'm not the fanatical type. I have doubt in my mind about it. Maybe I believe half.

"But I have a sick wife. She's been comatose for twenty-seven months. I believe she's gonna wake up. Twenty-seven months. You've gotta believe it or you'll go off your nut. I'm looking at a tree across the street. That didn't get there by accident. I didn't get there by accident.

"They got all these shrines, the Blessed Mother, they have these sites in Yugoslavia. People go five, six times a year. Maybe there's nothing up there in the sky. But I'm going to go, just for the experience. If there's nothing there, I'd be satisfied. I've got nothing to lose."

O'BOYLE'S COULD BE SAID TO BE A ROMAN Catholic way of thinking or a Christian-American way of thinking—or both. There are, and forever have been, many who would deride him.

To put it baldly if not heartlessly, the notion of miracles has, since antiquity, had more than its fair share of naysayers, some of them the very smartest among us at any given point in time. Aristotle, Spinoza, Hume and Kierkegaard were not only men dedicated to scientific principles, but each considered it important to address the topic of miracles and insisted that natural law had no comfortable room for them. In our own day, atheists and agnostics would not apply the word *miracle* to anything except the über-secular ninth-inning rally or 60-yard Hail Mary pass, or perhaps the results of last month's Powerball lottery—miraculous for one person, a loss for millions. Even drifting back once again into the rightly revered history of our nation, we run up against such abject skeptics as Thomas Jefferson.

As already discussed, our Founding Fathers were largely of a rationalist bent. But this is not to say they were unreligious, not at all. Jefferson, obviously one of the finest thinkers in their midst, dwelled deeply and often on God—and on Jesus Christ. There is a book kept in print today that is called *The Jefferson Bible.* It isn't a rewriting but a reediting of the New Testament. Jefferson felt Christ to be perhaps the greatest teacher and philosopher who ever lived, and he tried to follow Jesus's precepts when concocting his own vision for a modern democracy (the slave issue notwithstanding). But he did not follow his personal devotion to Jesus any further than in earthly matters; he didn't believe in miracles, and he didn't think Jesus's story needed the support of miracles to give it significance. So he took out his scissors. He sliced from the Gospels all supernatural occurrences, then pasted together the remaining lessons and words. His condensed book was one that he read all the time, and it contented and bolstered him.

How does the rationalist grapple with the magical thinker, especially if they are wrestling within one psyche? It's a good question and sometimes a terrible question.

It's one that I, as an editor, once posed to the fine writer Tom Junod, who as mentioned earlier, had written, and brilliantly, about Medjugorje for LIFE. A true professional, he had not approached from the "personal" side in that feature, but I knew that when he had traveled to Yugoslavia for us in the early 1990s, personal matters were very much on his mind. I subsequently put together a slim book of meditations about Mary, who has long been such a central figure when regarding the miraculous, and I asked Tom if he might write about his own experiences in reporting that story. He was happy to do so.

"I made a trip to Medjugorje in April 1991," Junod recalled for the 1997 book *Blessed Art Thou Among Women: Reflections on Mary in Our World Today.* "I went as a journalist, but also as a wobbly Catholic, who, although balanced near the end of belief, still believed that Mary could *do* it, if I called upon her with true heart." Junod and his wife did have a petition to Mary at that time—for a baby—and so they were much like many others heading for Medjugorje, even if they were also different from many of the others. "On the evening of my 33rd birthday, I met up with a group of pilgrims—people call themselves pilgrims, rather than tourists, when they go to Medjugorje—at Kennedy Airport, and when they began their incessant chanting of the

**Moses with the Ten Commandments,** ***a 1659 painting by Rembrandt that is housed today in the Gemäldegalerie in Berlin.***

ALEXANDRA BOULAT/VII/CORBIS

Rosary, I forced myself to join in, even though I hadn't said the Rosary in something like 15 years, and had forgotten some of the more esoteric creeds."

Junod wrote with great good humor, but always with a large measure of not only sympathy but insight: insight into not only the general human condition but his own. He said that he was "superstitious" in regard to the Virgin, yet he found himself reciting those Hail Marys, over and over, "to fool myself, to fool *her,* and once I made myself say it, I didn't *stop* saying it, and for 10 days its words bent and shaped my lips."

He later wrote: "I didn't *get* it, myself. The word: I didn't hear it, and so, of course, I didn't get it—I wasn't healed. I prayed, but I wasn't *convinced.* I didn't start the trip believing, and I didn't end the trip believing . . . [A]t night, when the famished pilgrims marched into the barbed mountains to garner their messages from Mary, I clung close to Carol, to find out if she ever heard what she needed to hear, and to find out, for myself, what in the world that might be."

In talking to Tom at the time and then receiving his writing, it became so clear to me: There are very many of us, even in our postmodern age, who can be scientific—clinical—about the possibilities of miracles, yet who, when push comes to shove, want to, or need to . . . if not believe, at least wonder.

Something strange did happen before Tom and Carol left Medjugorje. There are various supernatural occurrences, besides the visits to the visionaries, that have been associated with that place since 1981, and Junod wrote about one for my book on Mary: "I saw a miracle, on one of my last days there. Toward sunset, I went along to the west side of the big church, and there I saw hundreds of pilgrims staring gaspingly at the sun, in the belief that it had started to spin. The Miracle of the Sun, this is called—and I *saw* it, by God. No, I don't think the sun was spinning, exactly; but you could look at it, and you didn't have to worry about burning your eyes. These were the last days of Yugoslavia; the last days before the secession of Croatia; the last days before the raw bloody birth of Bosnia; the last days before the massacres; the last days before the ethnic cleansings . . . and now at the last of this day there was a sun in the sky shorn of its barbed heat, and recast as an emblem of mercy. It was a sun that *invited* you to look at it: an acid-trippy sun, a sun that seemed to pulse with pity—a *personal* sun, just as the Christian God is said to be a personal God. I did not gasp, however, and I did not fall to my knees, and I did not renew my old pledge of fealty to Mary. I had asked her for a miracle, and although she had given me one, it wasn't the miracle I wanted, and it wasn't miracle enough."

DIFFERENT RELIGIOUS TRADITIONS, BEYOND just Catholicism, have sanctioned miracles in their histories, but in some cases the passage of time has altered their stances concerning miracles. To look but briefly at the Judeo-Christian tradition, of which the Judeo is the older half: The Christian Old Testament is derived from the Hebrew Tanakh; the kinds of miracles recounted therein, familiar to the faithful of either flock, well illustrate the Jewish view of miracles—they are ancient events that happened, as saving graces, precisely at the needed moment. Sarah, a 90-year-old woman, becomes pregnant and gives birth to Isaac; a sea miraculously parts; food drops from the heavens; priests blow rams' horns, the Israelites shout and the walls of the Jericho fortress tumble; Joshua asks for the sun to stop so he can defeat his enemies; Daniel survives the lion's den; a whale does not consume Jonah; Elisha cures leprosy; Elijah raises the dead. Wrathfully (but with purpose): Swarms of ills beset the intransigent Egyptians; the earth swallows up those who conspire against Moses and Aaron; the idolatrous who dared to build a golden calf succumb to plague; Sodomites, Gomorrites, Canaanites, Amorites and Assyrians are smote.

We don't, however, see overt miracles in Judaism in the time after that recounted in the Bible. In the Talmud—which was compiled between the second and sixth centuries—it is evident that the era of miracles has passed. Miracles don't figure much at all in current mainstream Judaism. While Reform, Reconstructionist and Conservative Jews still offer prayers to God for healing or help, they are not praying for miracles but for good things to happen. The Hasidim and some Orthodox still believe in the possibility of miracles, but the religion as a whole does not subscribe.

But then there's this, which is yet another thing that leads back to the question of what is a miracle: While miraculous *moments* for the Jews generally stopped when the Bible story ended, the very survival of the race is seen as an overarchingly miraculous event. During the Passover Seder, Jews recall how despite hundreds of years of servitude they escaped that hellish Egyptian desert and made it to the Land of Milk and Honey. Some Haggadoth spin it forward and discuss how the Jews endured not just the persecutions of the tyrant Pharaoh but also those of the Greeks, the Romans, the Persians, the Spanish, the Russians and the Nazis. In less than a decade German leader Adolf Hitler helped wipe out two thirds of European Jewry, yet three years after the end of World War II, bands of Jewish soldiers fought off the combined forces of Egypt, Jordan, Iraq, Syria, Lebanon and Saudi Arabia.

As David Ben-Gurion, Israel's founding prime minister, noted: "A Jew who does not believe in miracles is not a realist." His, as you might guess, considering the long and oft-tortured history of the faith, was not an original thought. Leo Tolstoy called the Jew "the emblem of eternity. He whom neither slaughter nor torture of thousands of years could destroy, he whom neither fire nor sword nor Inquisition was able to wipe off the face of the earth." Isn't such survival, and the very existence of Israel in the 21st century, miraculous? Mark Twain wrote that while Jews are small in number—what he called "a nebulous dim puff of stardust lost in the blaze of the Milky Way"—they "saw them all, beat them all." And when the French king Louis XIV asked the philosopher and mathematician Blaise Pascal to offer proof of miracles, Pascal simply answered: "Why, the Jews, Your Majesty—the Jews."

***In November 2006, two faithful kneel in the Basilica of the Annunciation in Nazareth, northern Israel, where, it is said, the Virgin Mary was visited by the Angel Gabriel and learned her blessed fate.***

NATAN DVIR/POLARIS

There are miracles, and then Miracles. There are specific apparitions and oddly behaving stars, and then there are the Jews, Creation itself, Nature, Human Evolution and the Opposable Thumb, the Continued Existence of the Blue Whale and of the Crocodile, the Triumph of American Democracy. That's the thing about the world we live in, isn't it? Every day might deliver something strange or inexplicable, and it could be quite a small thing—a daffodil, a kind word at the right moment, the migration of the monarch butterfly—which we accept and therefore almost don't notice until we pause to ask: Did God have a hand in that, too? Or *the* hand?

What part of it all is miraculous? Just the beginning? The day-to-day?

As we go forward in these pages, we will narrow our focus. "The miraculous" is hardly a topic that can be conveniently synopsized, nor can it be documented in a series of images. It's bigger than that. What can be discussed (and shown) further, after having talked about the whole of it—the "it" being miracles as they are important to God-worshiping people—are individual miracles, as trusted by many people, even multitudes. These will include the long ago—Moses's miracles and Jesus's—and the up-to-date, such as Medjugorje.

Not all of them will be from the Catholic realm. We will address, in words and pictures, the miracles that are important to the history of many faiths. And after the old, there is always the new. In the past two centuries in American religious history, the miraculous has played a crucial role in, for instance, the founding or rise of Mormonism, Protestant evangelicalism and Pentecostalism, the latter of which is an American-born faith that today represents one of the world's fastest-growing religious movements.

But, yes, we will talk of Catholic subjects, since Mary has long been seen in that church as an ultimate miracle worker, and for many people, including outsiders, Rome remains the home repository, and even the arbiter, of the miraculous faith.

In 1858 in Lourdes, a village in the French Pyrenees, Our Lady appeared to Bernadette Soubirous. In 1917, Our Lady greeted, continuously over a period of six months, three shepherd children in Fátima. In our day, she perhaps counseled the visionaries of Medjugorje. It should be noted that these things are never to be taken casually or cavalierly. In the past nearly two centuries, the Church has approved—using a scrupulous investigative process—several apparitions that merit "pious belief." That's hardly many, and the apparition at Medjugorje is not yet one of them, but the Church is saying that even if we deal not in faith but cold, calculated definition, we still must deal with miracles.

It always comes down to this, doesn't it: Do you believe?

***On April 30, 2005, Irineos I, Patriarch of Jerusalem, is borne aloft during the Greek Orthodox Easter ceremony of the Holy Fire in the Church of the Holy Sepulchre, said by many Christians to be on the site of Jesus's final resting place.***

## FLEEING PHARAOH

Several of the most dramatic miracles in the Hebrew Bible involve the persecution and flight of Moses and his people, the Jews, from Egypt, which occurred perhaps between 1300 and 1200 B.C. Shadowing them constantly was Pharaoh, and constantly on the horizon outside Cairo they were reminded of his might whenever they espied the Great Pyramid of the tyrannical Khufu, who ruled for some two dozen years during the Fourth Dynasty (2575–2465 B.C.).

# Old Testament

## Miracles

*There is a qualitative difference between the miracles of ancient Hebrew scripture and those of the New Testament. All miracles see God visiting the earthly realm and influencing human affairs. But in the Old Testament, He seems interested in nation building: His miracles, be they concerned with human salvation itself (his instructions to Noah), the deliverance of overarching principles (the Ten Commandments) or assists in war (the Plagues of Egypt and the destruction of the Egyptian army), are directed at his "people." In the New Testament, by contrast, the miracles are Christ-centered and much more "personal"—a fantastic birth, a healing, an exorcism, a resurrection. As far as Christianity is concerned, the story is built properly: God makes the world, protects the world from above, God reenters the world through His son in order to save humanity. He cannot do these things without being witnessed; and so, early on, we have Him speaking directly to and guiding Abraham, and then we have His stunning, earthshaking relationship with Moses.*

LIZ GILBERT/REDUX

ERICH LESSING/ART RESOURCE, NY (2)

## FROM A BURNING BUSH

To the Jews he is Moshe Rabbeinu (Moses Our Teacher), lawgiver, hero above all heroes; to Christians he is a model of faith; to Muslims, Musa is the first prophet to herald the coming of Muhammad. He is said to have lived some 3,200 years ago, in the time of the Egyptian pharaoh Ramses II. Proving his existence has been, as with Abraham and the other Hebrew Bible patriarchs, impossible. But what is written in scripture depicts Moses as exceedingly human: both weak and strong, brave yet tormented by doubt, a rebel but a faithful follower. "The most solitary and most powerful hero in biblical history," Elie Wiesel has called Moses. "After him, nothing else was the same again."

He began life as a Hebrew born during a time of persecution; his mother tried hiding her infant boy, but before long she grew desperate and left him in a small boat by the water's edge. The baby was rescued by Pharaoh's daughter and raised as her son. So life in Egypt was hardly bad for Moses—adopted scion in Pharaoh's family, after all—but it was meanwhile intolerable for his blood kinsmen, and God would summon Moses back to their side. From Exodus, Chapter 3: "And the angel of the Lord appeared unto him in a flame of fire out of the midst of a bush; and he looked, and, behold, the bush burned with fire, and the bush was not consumed. And Moses said, I will now turn aside, and see this great sight, why the bush is not burnt. And when the Lord saw that he turned aside to see, God called unto him out of the midst of the bush, and said Moses, Moses . . . And Moses hid his face; for he was afraid to look upon God." Yet he was emboldened by God, and soon was challenging Pharaoh on His behalf: "Let my people go." At left: The Sinai Desert, through which the Israelites passed and in which Moses saw the burning bush. In fact, some at the Holy Monastery of St. Catherine in the Sinai claim that the thorn bush seen above is the very one.

## PLAGUING PHARAOH

When Moses, accompanied by his brother, Aaron, demanded freedom for his people, "Pharaoh said, Who is the Lord, that I should obey His voice to let Israel go? I know not the Lord, neither will I let Israel go." Well, he was about to come to know God only too well. God (to Israel: Yahweh) used Moses as his constant agent in inflicting what are alternately called the Plagues of Egypt or the Ten Plagues. The first was the Plague of Blood, in which Moses was told to touch the waters of the Nile (above) with the tip of his staff: "This is what the Lord says: By this you will know that I am the Lord: With the staff that is in my hand I will strike the water of the Nile, and it will be changed into blood. The fish in the Nile will die, and the river will stink and thus the Egyptians will not be able to drink its water." The Plague of Frogs, initiated by Aaron and Moses (opposite, top), followed: "This is what the great Lord says: Let my people go, so that they may worship me. If you refuse to let them go, I will plague your whole country with frogs. The Nile will teem with frogs. They will come up into your palace and your bedroom and onto your bed." Following were plagues of lice, flies, diseased livestock, boils, hail, locusts, darkness and finally human death (opposite, bottom): "On that same night I will pass through Egypt and strike down every firstborn—both men and animals—and I will bring judgment on all the gods of Egypt. I am the Lord." Pharaoh finally relented and set free the Israelites, spurring the Exodus.

JOHN CUMBERLAND/IMAGE SOURCE/AURORA

HULTON/GETTY

LEBRECHT MUSIC & ARTS/CORBIS

KENNETH GARRETT/NATIONAL GEOGRAPHIC CREATIVE/GETTY

GRANGER

**OUT OF EGYPT**

Now began the flight of the Israelites. They had the Egyptians pursuing them, but were always guided and bolstered by their all-powerful ally. "God led the people about, through the way of the wilderness of the Red Sea: and the children of Israel went up harnessed out of the land of Egypt." The words in Hebrew are actually *yam suf,* meaning "sea of reeds" rather than "Red Sea," as the term is mistakenly rendered in the King James and other versions of the Bible. (We use the semi-archaic King James translation in this LIFE volume, if only because we feel the sheer poetry of the language is such a fine match

for the subject matter and for the photography.)

So, Red Sea, sea of reeds: Where is it that the climactic event of the Israelites' escape happened, when "Moses stretched out his hand over the sea; and the Lord caused the sea to go back by a strong east wind all that night, and made the sea dry land, and the waters were divided"? We don't know for sure which body of water between Egypt and the Sinai is referred to. Sea of reeds: It could have been the marshland at the southernmost shore of the Mediterranean Sea—Lake Timsah of the Bitter Lakes. Or maybe it was the Red Sea after all, for Exodus makes clear, as do centuries of artists (and now, decades of moviemakers) interpreting the scene (the engraving here is after a painting by Gustave Doré), that the crossing was truly awesome: "And the children of Israel went into the midst of the sea upon the dry ground: and the waters were a wall unto them on their right hand, and on their left." Then, of course, as Doré shows us, God let those walls collapse and let the Egyptians have it, as the Israelites sped on to the Sinai Peninsula.

Above is a second picture of the Holy Monastery of St. Catherine (please see page 23) nestled at the base of Mount Sinai. This oldest continuously operating Christian monastery in the world sits upon the site of many dramatic events. Atop that mountain (if it was, as tradition holds, this particular mountain), God bequeathed to Moses, and thence to his people, the Ten Commandments, which comprise the rules for a moral life.

From Exodus 13:21: “And the Lord went before them by day in a pillar of cloud, to lead them along the way.” He was leading them perhaps south through Shur to the mountainous southern tip of the Sinai Peninsula and then north and up the eastern side to Canaan, to the Promised Land (that term has been at the heart of Jewish-Arab difficulties for centuries—promised to whom?). The gradual anointment of this as the “official” path of Exodus was begun in the fourth century A.D., when Saint Helena built a chapel in the Sinai highlands; other pilgrims followed, and other monasteries, churches and monuments arose.

But there is more than tradition at work here. One reason scholars think the southernmost route toward the peninsula’s tip is the likely candidate is because a trek through the Sinai’s nearly waterless interior would have left the Hebrews in critical danger of dying of thirst. Even still, miracles were needed. The barren landscape of the Wilderness of Shur, where they wandered for three days, left Moses and his 600,000 followers hungry and parched. When they arrived at the oasis of Marah, the water was

BPK, BERLIN/HUNGARIAN NATIONAL GALLERY/ALFREDO DAGLI ORTI/ART RESOURCE, NY

ERICH LESSING/ART RESOURCE, NY

not potable, but Moses was able to make it clean and sweet by striking a rock, and his people drank their fill. At the next stop, in Elim, they found a paradise of shade and water that fortified them before encountering a second wilderness—the Wilderness of Sin. Many in the flock "murmured against Moses." But God told Moses to promise them divine sustenance—"I will rain bread from heaven for you; and the people shall go out and gather a certain rate every day"—and it was provided. (Opposite: From the 15th-century Bohemian school, *Miracle of the Manna in the Desert and Moses Striking the Rock.*)

When Moses performed at the oasis, he made a crucial, and very human, mistake. He neglected to credit the true maker of the miracle, the Lord his God. For this transgression (or at least, this error of omission) he would retain the duty of leading his people to the border of the Promised Land, while being forbidden himself from ever entering. The mountain in the region (called Moab) where Moses gazed for the first and last time upon Canaan was called Nebo, and below is the vista in which Moses perhaps saw the Israelites' vast nation of tents spread out, as his people anticipated their deliverance.

# The Miracles of Jesus

*There were more large-scale Hebrew Bible miracles after those involving Moses: Joshua at Jericho, David from boyhood onward, Solomon and the God-blessed rise of Jerusalem. And then followed the life of Jesus of Nazareth, arguably the most important person in human history. Also: the greatest miracle worker of all time. The first miracle of Jesus belonged, of course, to God: the bequeathing of His son to mankind through the Immaculate Conception. The last miracle, too, would be the Father's: calling Jesus home through the Resurrection. Between these, based upon the record in the four Gospels of the New Testament (those of Mark, Matthew, Luke and John), Jesus Himself performed more than 35 miracles, that being a baseline for what anyone would consider miraculous. Only one miracle, the feeding of five thousand people by transforming five loaves and two fish into a bounty, appears in all Gospels; a dozen are so-called "three-Gospel miracles"; five more are in two Gospels; and the rest, including several famous miracles, are recounted only once each. In total, they speak to the awesomeness—in the literal sense—of Jesus Christ.*

CHRISTOPHER ANDERSON/MAGNUM

## IN THE LAND OF MARY AND JOSEPH

A nomadic Bedouin wanders in the Judaean desert east of Bethlehem in Israel, much as Bedouins and Jewish shepherds did two millennia ago when Jesus was born. That nativity happened perhaps in Bethlehem, although some scholars say Nazareth. The baby's earthly father was a carpenter named Joseph, and his mother was Joseph's wife, Mary. Much of Jesus's ministry would take place in this stark locale, and He or the entire family would travel in the desert several times to and from Jerusalem—beginning almost immediately after His birth. Many of Jesus's miracles were performed in Judaea.

## THE NATIVITY

The miracle in this critical part of the story is the Immaculate Conception, which is depicted on the opposite page in a 17th-century painting of that title by Il Guercino. Mary was at home when visited by the Angel Gabriel, who informed her that she had received the Holy Spirit and become pregnant. Joseph, in a dream, was also visited by the angel of the Lord, who spoke to him of his future wife's condition (please see page 77 in our chapter "The Miracles of the Saints"). And so it was that Mary was with child by God the Father.

Before she could give birth, the Roman ruler of the territory, Caesar Augustus, proclaimed that all people must register in the city of their origin (for what scholars now say was either a tax or a census). A simple tradesman like Joseph and his wife would never have dreamed of disobeying such an edict from on high, and so, despite Mary's state, they prepared to leave their home in Nazareth: "And Joseph also went up from Galilee, out of the city of Nazareth, into Judaea."

Today when we celebrate Christmas, little thought is given to Joseph and Mary's arduous 100-mile journey from Nazareth to Bethlehem. The Gospels provide few details, but research by archaeologists and biblical scholars enables us to envision the route taken by the couple through the Holy Land. By the end of the first day of their odyssey, they would have passed the Sea of Galilee, which would of course be the setting for many seminal events, including many miracles, in their son's remarkable life. (Thirty years after his parents skirted the sea, Jesus would preach the Sermon on the Mount there.) On the fifth day of their journey, Mary and Joseph trekked westward through the Judaean desert, a treacherous wilderness populated mostly by Bedouin shepherds. Its dangers included mountain lions, vipers, scorpions and marauding bandits. As Joseph and Mary approached Jerusalem, they likely confronted gruesome evidence of Roman tyranny—such as burned villages and toppled crosses that were used to crucify rebellious Jews. For these pilgrims, however, the hardships of the road melted away the moment they entered the city. An ancient psalm well describes the spiritual elation that devout Jews like Mary and Joseph would have experienced when they first came to the summit of the Mount of Olives: "Let my tongue cleave to the roof of my mouth; if I prefer not Jerusalem above my chief joy."

ERICH LESSING/ART RESOURCE, NY

The focus of Mary and Joseph's visit to Jerusalem would have been the Holy Temple where, after taking their required ritual baths, they would have made their sacrifice—probably two turtle doves. After leaving the Temple, they completed the short five-mile trip to Bethlehem by nightfall. The unusually high number of visitors to the little town had filled the local inn to capacity, so they sought refuge in a grotto, one of the many used by shepherds for thousands of years as shelters from predators and cold weather. Through the two pictures on this page—one grand and one stark—perhaps we can envision the Nativity. The painting, made in the 15th century by Fra Angelico, depicts the adoration of the Magi—the kings—who were beckoned by a star to come and pay tribute (one of several miracles that night: the star, the herald angels, the birth itself). The photograph, made in modern times for LIFE by Denis Waugh, is of a grotto that has indeed been used by shepherds for centuries. It is located about two miles from the traditional site of Jesus's birth.

DENIS WAUGH

## BEGINNING HIS MISSION

Above we see the Pool of Bethesda in Jerusalem, still flaunting its healthful, perhaps healing waters in the mid–19th century—as it does today. It was the site of a famous miracle of Jesus, this one from the Gospel of John, which is seen as a biography independent of the Synoptic, interrelated Gospels of Mark, Matthew and Luke. John has Jesus encountering a paralytic man near the comforting baths. The man explains that he can never get therapy because his condition always makes him late in line. Jesus immediately heals the man, who rises and walks.

On the opposite page are two pictures—one a painting from the 19th century by Julius Schnorr von Carolsfeld and the other a photograph made not long after—depicting events at Cana, which was certainly in today's Israel though it is not known precisely where (the photograph was made in present-day Kefr Kenna, which stakes a claim to having been Cana). Jesus attended a wedding there, and, as recounted in John 2:11, sought to establish Himself: "This beginning of miracles did Jesus in Cana of Galilee, and manifested forth His glory; and His disciples believed on Him." What had happened: Jesus, having been baptized by John around A.D. 26, began His own evangelical ministry in Galilee. He lectured in synagogues. According to Luke, His hometown congregants rejected Him, and He took His preaching to villages on the western shore of the Sea of Galilee. There He began building a team of disciples, starting with two pairs of brothers, all fishermen: Peter and Andrew, John and James ("I will make you fishers of men"). Jesus's flock was becoming well known in the region, and since there was talk of His being the one presaged by John the Baptist, there was a growing urgency for Him to prove Himself—not least to His lieutenants. One day in Cana, a village north of Nazareth, Jesus and His mother were at a feast. When the wine ran out, Mary brought the news to Jesus. Jesus ordered "six waterpots of stone" filled with water. He promptly turned the liquid into wine. In a later episode at Cana, Jesus heard about a dying boy and healed him. He was proving His divinity.

FRANCIS FRITH/MARY EVANS PICTURE LIBRARY

THE GALLERY COLLECTION/CORBIS

UNDERWOOD & UNDERWOOD/CORBIS

RICHARD T. NOWITZ/CORBIS

NATIONAL GALLERY, LONDON/ART RESOURCE, NY

RMN-GRAND PALAIS/ART RESOURCE, NY

## THE MIRACLE WORKER

Jesus performed different kinds of miracles once He had embarked upon His ministry. In fact, His miracles can be categorized. What are called Miraculous Feedings is a subset, as is Nature Miracles. The largest grouping is Healings, Resurrections (not His own) and Exorcisms. The only miracle reported in all four Gospels is the feeding of the five thousand. Three Gospels agree on a leper being cleansed, Peter's ill mother-in-law being cured, a group of possessed people being healed, the calming of the Sea of Galilee, demons being cast into a herd of pigs, the healing of the paralytic, the raising of Jairus's daughter (Jesus's first resurrection), the healing of a woman with hemorrhages, the healing of a man's withered hand, the walking on water on the Sea of Galilee, an epileptic boy and then a blind man being cured. Matthew and Luke agree that a Roman centurion's slave was healed, and Matthew and Mark have accounts of the Gentile woman's daughter recovering, as well as the story of four thousand being fed (a different episode than the five thousand, but still with loaves and fish) and a fig tree withering after having been cursed. Mark and Luke both write of an unclean spirit being cast out. Among the several one-Gospel miracles there are everything from the Cana water-into-wine event (in John) to several healings (even of a royal official's son, also in John) to the raising of Lazarus from the dead (again in John) to an unexpectedly good day of fishing (in Luke). This brief catalog is offered so that the reader might have some basic contextual background for the wondrous biblical stories you know and remember.

On the opposite page are the ruins of a synagogue at Capernaum, a city on the shore of the Sea of Galilee. Jesus may have preached here; He certainly spent much time evangelizing in Capernaum. Per miracle, this may have been His most active site, starting with a miraculous catch of fish (the net was about to break and Jesus's friends had to enlist another boat) and progressing through the ministering to Peter's mother-in-law, then to a paralytic, then to a woman with a bleeding condition. He raised Jairus's daughter here, healed two blind men and a mute demoniac, and fixed the withered hand. Most important, surely, He spoke His transcendent Sermon on the Mount to the people of Capernaum and nearby precincts.

Two of Jesus's most famous miracles are depicted in the paintings above: *Christ Healing the Paralytic at the Pool of Bethesda,* by Bartolomé Esteban Murillo, and *Christ and the Multiplication of the Loaves and the Fish,* by Gaspard de Crayer.

There is little question that the Gospel writers, who were trying to spread the Word—often clandestinely—in the decades after Christ died, were trying to establish His divinity. They were propagandists for what would become Christianity.

But there is so much on the table. There are so many stories, such detail and such corroboration, that even a scientific, secular appraisal has to be: This was a spiritual man. An altogether extraordinary man.

BPK, BERLIN/HAMBURGER KUNSTHALLE/ELKE WALFORD/ART RESOURCE, NY

## AT—AND ON—THE SEA OF GALILEE

Located 16 miles east of Nazareth, it is not a sea at all but a 64-square-mile lake in a depression of the Jordan River (in fact, at more than 600 feet below sea level, Lake Tiberias, seen here, is the lowest freshwater lake in the world). In Jesus's day it supported vibrant cities—Capernaum and Bethsaida each had more than 15,000 residents—as well as many smaller fishing villages. This is the place where Jesus's mission was nurtured and launched: Five of His 12 disciples were from towns along its shores (and Mary Magdalene came from a Galilean village as well); the great majority of His three dozen recorded miracles were performed by, or on, this sea. Here, He turned the meager ration of bread and fish into a meal for a multitude, and here, he calmed the waters (in the painting above, by Philipp Otto Runge, where he walks on its surface, he also calms Peter). He preached often and effectively by its waters. He used a fishing net to show what Judgment Day would be like, when all humankind will be gathered up.

Nearby, He delivered to the throng (His fame was growing) the Sermon on the Mount, an ethical lesson for the ages: "Blessed are the meek: for they shall inherit the earth . . . Blessed are the merciful: for they shall obtain mercy. Blessed are the pure in heart: for they shall see God. Blessed are the peacemakers: for they shall be called the children of God . . ."

It was Augustine who later labeled this lesson the Sermon on the Mount. In Matthew's Gospel the sermon extends to 100 verses, and scholars speculate that it was pieced together by the writer as sort of a Jesus 101 teaching. It goes on from the blessed-are's to "You are the Salt of the earth" and "You are the light of the world," then to an explication of important commandments (those against murder and adultery) and a refutation of the ages-old, revenge-fueled equation "an eye for an eye and a tooth for a tooth." It includes the Lord's Prayer: "Our Father which art in Heaven/Hallowed be thy name . . ." In the Gospel of Luke, the speech is just less than a third as long, and delivered on flat ground after Jesus returns from the summit. The messages are the same.

Jesus's teachings themselves were miraculous; and that they were preserved and led to the establishment of the world's largest religion, with 2 billion Christian faithful today, is miraculous. The notion of giving one's cloak to a needy neighbor had no currency at all in the violent, grasping age and place in which Jesus moved. His thinking was not merely radical, as has often been said; it was impossible. It was sensational.

But it represented a new and, to the poor, attractive way. Despite many efforts to erase it in the decades and centuries to follow, it endured. A miracle.

RENE BURRI/MAGNUM

SCALA/ART RESOURCE, NY

## THE RESURRECTION OF LAZARUS

Very few miracles are as riveting in the telling as life after death. In our day, there are many witnesses who have, they say, seen "the other side"—sometimes represented by bright lights and sometimes by darkness. Historically, the best-known resurrection is Jesus's own. Second is probably that of Lazarus: "Then Jesus six days before the Passover came to Bethany, where Lazarus was which had been dead, whom He raised from the dead."

Today the small village of Bethany, on the outskirts of Jerusalem, is known by the Arabic name el-Azariyeh, meaning "place of Lazarus." He was Jesus's dear friend, and Jesus visited Lazarus and his sisters, Mary and Martha, several times at their house there; in fact, Bethany is sometimes referred to as Jesus's Judaean home. When, at one point, the sisters informed Jesus, "Lord, behold, he whom Thou lovest is sick," Jesus quickly determined to go and help Lazarus, who was gravely ill. His disciples were concerned, as Jesus's growing ministry had been making fresh enemies, and they warned Him against the trip: "Master, the Jews of late sought to stone Thee; and goest Thou thither again?" Jesus insisted: "Our friend Lazarus sleepest; but I go, that I may awake him out of sleep."

He did go to the tomb in Bethany (opposite), and He did raise the dead Lazarus and restore him to life (above, in a 17th-century painting by Il Guercino). But He did not do Himself much good with this extraordinary act: "Then many of the Jews which came to Mary, and had seen the things which Jesus did, believed on Him. But some of them went their ways to the Pharisees, and told them what things Jesus had done . . . If we let Him thus alone, all men will believe on Him: and the Romans shall come and take away both our place and nation." Things were getting hot for Jesus, and they were getting hottest whenever he ventured near Jerusalem.

RICHARD T. NOWITZ/CORBIS

ERICH LESSING/ART RESOURCE, NY

SCALA/ART RESOURCE, NY

## REVEALING HIMSELF

The Transfiguration remains one of the most mysterious of the miracles associated with Jesus, and that claim is made while accepting the notion that any miracle is plenty mysterious. Along with the Immaculate Conception and Jesus's own Resurrection, it is a miracle not obviously wrought by Jesus Himself, but by God. As with earlier miracles, it was clearly done with the intention of further convincing and inspiring Jesus's cadre of friends and followers—the trio of disciples, Peter, James and John, accompanying Him to the mountaintop and those waiting below who would subsequently be told: Believe it, this is the Son of God.

In John's Gospel, it occurred as follows: Before Jesus's final journey to Jerusalem, an extraordinary thing happened in the center of Galilee on a summit just outside of Capernaum—a rounded summit traditionally believed to be that of Mount Tabor, seen at left. He drew Peter, James and John aside and led "them up into an high mountain apart by themselves and He was transfigured before them. And His raiment became shining, exceeding white as snow; so as no fuller on earth can white them."

It's all so magical and open to interpretation; it is not a message spoken but shown. On the mountain, they prayed, and as they did so, Jesus was somehow transformed—*transfigured* is the word the Bible uses to describe what occurred. He glowed, and then was visited by Moses and Elijah, who talked to Him. Then there came a cloud, and from the cloud a voice: "This is my beloved Son: hear Him."

And then it was over. The men descended, and Jesus asked His friends to keep what they had seen secret until the "Son of man" had risen from the dead. (Good luck with keeping the secret.)

What did the Transfiguration of Jesus (above, in a 16th-century painting by Titian) mean? It was yet another miracle that should have removed any lingering doubts about Jesus's divinity harbored by Peter, James or John. But in Luke's Gospel there is one thing more. Luke wrote that Moses and Elijah "spake of His decease which He should accomplish at Jerusalem." These words presage the Passion of Jesus that lay ahead.

RICHARD T. NOWITZ/CORBIS

UNIVERSAL HISTORY ARCHIVE/GETTY

## THE PASSION AND RESURRECTION

Another of Jesus's best-known miracles occurred outside Jericho. En route to Jerusalem as Passover was approaching, Jesus, traveling with His disciples—this time to meet His ultimate fate—either paused on the way into the city to heal a blind man by the side of the road (according to the Gospel of Luke), healed the man upon exiting the city (says Mark) or healed not one but two blind beggars (according to Matthew). Regardless, Jesus now knew who He was, where He was headed, and also what He represented and what He could do. As He eloquently put it to the blind man in Mark's Gospel, "thy faith hath made thee whole."

In Jerusalem, many who had heard that Jesus was arriving rushed out to meet Him "and cried, Hosanna: Blessed is the King of Israel that cometh in the name of the Lord." Jesus, seeing the glorious city stretching out before Him, wept.

Then, according to the Gospel of Mark, He leaped quickly into action, casting the moneylenders out of the Temple ("Is it not written, My house shall be called of all nations the house of prayer? But ye have made it a den of thieves") and continuing to preach in parables, defying His enemies to take Him. They didn't, at first. But Joseph Caiaphas, the high priest in Jerusalem, had determined that Jesus must go, and was watching events proceed, looking for his moment: "The chief priests, and the scribes sought how they might take Him by craft, and put Him to death." *By craft.* And craft's name would be Judas. And the place would be in the Garden of Gethsemane (opposite), where Jesus—increasingly anxious and tormented—first asked God to relieve Him of His yoke—that "if it were possible, the hour might pass from Him"—and finally came to this: "Nevertheless not what I will, but what Thou wilt."

Jesus was condemned by the crowd as much as by Pontius Pilate, and was crucified. Those events were in no way miraculous; in fact, they were prosaic, political—the way of the cruel human world. But what happened next was as miraculous and consequential as anything that had occurred before or has since.

Above is a 17th-century painting by Jan Brueghel the Younger and Hendrick van Balen depicting the encounter between the risen Christ and Mary Magdalene, first to see the resurrected Jesus. ("The first day of the week cometh Mary Magdalene early, when it was yet dark, unto the sepulchre, and seeth the stone taken away from the sepulchre . . .") He would spend several more hours or a few more days on earth, and those hours or days, presented as evidence of His Resurrection and of His divinity, today stand as moments that formed the Western world.

## JESUS ASCENDS

The rise of Christ's Church was begun with His returning from the dead. But while He had risen, He had not yet ascended, and so His Passion still had unfinished business—not least, convincing the doubting disciples of His continuing presence and influence in the temporal world. This was necessary, because without their fervid belief in Him, there could be no evangelical movement. How could they spread the Word without faith in what had happened—and, indeed, was still happening?

According to Scripture, Jesus appeared to two disciples—one was Cleopas, the other perhaps was Luke—on the road to Emmaus on the very day of His Resurrection, having already been seen by Mary Magdalene. (Above: The 19th-century painting *Christ at Emmaus,* by Caroly Marko II.) As they walked, Jesus lectured the men on how the recent events were in fulfillment of

DE AGOSTINI/GETTY

NATIONAL GALLERY, LONDON/ART RESOURCE, NY

so much that had been predicted: "And beginning at Moses and all the prophets, he expounded unto them in all the Scriptures the things concerning Himself."

Jesus appeared next to Peter, then addressed the congregation of 11 apostles in what is known today as "the upper room"—more formally the Coenaculum or the Hall of the Last Supper—where Jesus's men gathered in private when in Jerusalem. As Jesus materialized there, the apostles were "terrified and affrighted," but Jesus "opened He their understanding." In some Gospels there were other meetings with His followers in other places at other times, but essentially His work was done, and theirs was begun. In the poetic Gospel of Luke, following the meeting in the upper room, "He led them out as far as to Bethany, and He lifted up His hands and blessed them. And it came to pass, while He blessed them, He was parted from them, and carried up into heaven." Above: *The Ascension,* painted by Jacopo di Cione circa 1370.

## LOURDES

Along with Mecca and Jerusalem, the French town of Lourdes is one of the world's best known sites of pilgrimage. The great majority of the faithful who venture each year to this village in the Pyrenees foothills are Catholic or Orthodox Christians. The Protestant denominations are less likely to believe in the miraculousness of the Virgin Mary and are hard-pressed to credit her apparitions—in Lourdes or other places. But those who do feel she appeared in Lourdes also feel that, one day, they must themselves get to Lourdes.

# The Great Pilgrimages

*It's a cycle: Faith allows one to believe in miracles . . . a belief in miracles inspires a more fervent faith . . . faith creates longing and a desire to draw closer . . . the site of a miracle becomes a point of focus . . . the pilgrim makes his or her way there and then, arriving, finds that faith and inspiration overflow. Everything increases. Many Christians want to visit Bethlehem or Nazareth in their lifetimes. A good many Jews need to bring themselves to Jerusalem, as do a good many Muslims, who are even more driven to make the hajj—the great pilgrimage to Mecca in Saudi Arabia. All around the world there are shrines, churches, temples, or simply limpid pools of serenity where nothing supernatural occurred (that we know of); these are places we go to for spiritual nourishment—on our own personal pilgrimages. And then there are the famous sites in Europe where the Virgin was said to appear, and where millions flock every year. Here and on the following pages is what some of the great pilgrimages look like. Even the images inspire.*

STEVE MCCURRY/MAGNUM

ALINARI/GETTY

## THE SONG OF BERNADETTE

In 1858, Lourdes was a quiet market town of perhaps 4,000 souls. It was attractively rustic and Pyrenean—it had an impressive castle—and was happy to cater to travelers headed into the mountains for recreation or the revivifying waters farther on at Bareges or Cauterets. If those destination burgs knew how things were about to change!

The Soubirous family included a 14-year-old girl named Bernadette. On February 11, 1858, she went walking all the way to the Grotto of Massabielle. She returned home that day with a remarkable story: a beautiful, shimmering lady had appeared to her. Bernadette ventured to the grotto again and, wonderfully, the lady came back as well. She spoke for the first time during Bernadette's third visit, which took place on February 18, and made it clear that she wished to counsel Bernadette personally and that there was no need to write things down—Bernadette would remember. The lady revealed herself as "the Immaculate Conception." This immediately translated into the Virgin Mary for the devout of Lourdes, and the story of Bernadette's vision spread.

Bernadette would visit with the Virgin 18 times in all; many of the later audiences were attended by hundreds of onlookers who could not see the apparition but were nonetheless moved. The lady told Bernadette about the value of love, penance, prayer and helping the poor. She urged Bernadette to ask the priests to build a chapel in the grotto, and this was done. It was only the beginning. On these pages: Bernadette in the grotto (far left); a portrait of her made circa 1863 (left); and a modern-day service in the grotto (below).

HERMANN BREDEHORST/POLARIS

THREE LIONS/GETTY

ALFRED EISENSTAEDT/LIFE/THE PICTURE COLLECTION

ABBAS/MAGNUM

## JOURNEYS FUELED BY FAITH AND HOPE

Today, Lourdes can still be called a town—population 15,000 or so—but it has more hotel rooms per square mile than any other French locale save Paris; it features some 270 hotels, and can accommodate around 5 million pilgrims each year. It has been estimated that more than 200 million faithful have visited the shrine in the grotto since 1860, and there are complicated reasons for this. One is that the Church in Rome, which had been considering miracles since time immemorial but hadn't been presented with one of these celebrated children-and-Mary cases, was not immediately suspicious or standoffish in regard to Lourdes. Consider: Bernadette was made a Roman Catholic saint in 1933, and the Mary-dedicated pope John Paul II twice went to Lourdes to pray. In 2007 his successor, Benedict XVI, authorized special indulgences connected with the upcoming 150th anniversary of

the first apparition. A more prosaic reason for Lourdes's allure in the 20th century and into the 21st: There was a hit Hollywood movie starring Jennifer Jones, *The Song of Bernadette,* made in 1943, and it still plays on cable every Easter season.

There was one more compelling factor, which over time attracted many pilgrims: It was said that the waters flowing from springs in the grotto had miraculous curative powers. Before Bernadette visited on that day in 1858, the villagers had been routinely dumping garbage and collecting firewood in the place, but in the wake of the furor, it became sacred ground—and then came the reports of the magical waters. People began blessing themselves with the water and people began gulping it down. The Roman Catholic Church itself, after what it considers stringent examination, has given the stamp of approval to 69 official miraculous healings at Lourdes. On these pages: Nurses assist the infirm during their visits to Lourdes in 1958 (opposite) and 1987 (above).

POLARIS

ARCHIVES CHARMET/BRIDGEMAN IMAGES

BETTMANN/CORBIS (2)

## OUR LADY OF FÁTIMA

*Worthy of belief* is the term decided upon by the Church in 1930 after a canonical inquiry into events that began transpiring in the Portuguese city of Fátima in 1917—events not wholly unlike those in Lourdes in France 59 years earlier, especially as they involved the apparition of a beautiful lady who has been generally identified as the Virgin Mary. Pope Benedict XVI certainly bolstered Rome's support—even though the Vatican does not insist or even ask that its faithful support apparitions—when in 2010 he visited Fátima and preached to 500,000 there. He talked about the place as a "maternal home" for Catholics and about John Paul II's belief that an "unseen hand" had perhaps saved his life during the 1981 assassination attempt in St. Peter's Square—an intercession John Paul always credited to Mary and allusively to Our Lady of Fátima, who most people see as one and the same.

This time there were three children, not one. There were multiple visits by the lady, as at Lourdes. Fátima's was a somewhat sterner Virgin. A mesmerizing new aspect was the delivery of three "secrets," which were warnings and prophecies from Mary that, in the event, did not all come true (while her vision of hell may or may not be subject to dispute, she predicted the assassination of a pope, which nearly happened but did not, and the Christian conversion of Soviet Russia), plus a supernatural addition in the odd behavior of the sun (which would also be part of the Medjugorje apparitions much later in the century).

On May 13, 1917, a trio of peasant children—Francisco and Jacinta Marto and their cousin Lucia Santos (seen at top, from left, at the site of the apparitions)—first saw the lady, but apparently there had been a prelude: visitations from an angel in 1916, who instructed them in specific prayers and sacrifices. On that day in May 1917, the adolescents were shepherding not far from their home in the village when, as Lucia, who would become a nun in her adulthood, later described it, they saw a woman "brighter than the sun, shedding rays of light clearer and stronger than a crystal ball filled with the most sparkling water and pierced by the burning rays of the sun."

The sun would continue to be part of this drama. The middle photo at left shows an audience on October 13, 1917 (the visitations were always on the 13th of the month), hoping to witness what has quickly become known as the Miracle of the Sun. At left, bottom, is a photograph, also made in 1917, that was printed in the official Vatican newspaper; it is said to show the sun in a position that would be "impossible" at 12:30 p.m. Far left: Pilgrims at the shrine, circa 1949.

EVELYN HOCKSTEIN/POLARIS (2)

## THE STORY OF LALIBELA

There are other great religious pilgrimages than those most famous in the Western world, and some of them have histories every bit as fascinating as those of Lourdes, Fátima or anywhere else. If they are not necessarily founded on a miracle—and some of them are—they are nonetheless miraculous in and of themselves, as their power to attract and inspire is an uncanny thing. Which brings us to the stone churches of Lalibela.

This is a city in northern Ethiopia: one of the holiest places in Africa and a center of pilgrimage for Ethiopian Orthodox Christians. Its reputation as a sacred center has a centuries-long history. In the 12th century, Lalibela was imagined as a New Jerusalem built in response to the capture of that city by Muslims led by Saladin in 1187. Many of Lalibela's historic buildings have names and layouts reflecting buildings in Jerusalem; the city's river is known as the River Jordan. Why? Why in the world?

Gebre Masqal Lalibela, for whom the city is named, was a member of the Zagwe Dynasty, which ruled Ethiopia in the 12th and 13th centuries, at which time Roha—the former name of the city of Lalibela—was the nation's capital. As the story goes, Gebre had spent good portions of his youth in Jerusalem

and the Holy Land before the Muslim conquest, and now he sought to build a place with similar—identical, even—civic and spiritual elements.

The Lalibela that evolved (perhaps 15,000 live there today) quickly became famous for its signature edifices: cruciform-shaped churches fashioned out of rock mountainsides or flat earth. Somehow, these structures combined the ancient, misty religiosity of such as England's Stonehenge, the air of the ancient clandestine Christian churches that existed under the radar of Roman persecution, and a cutting-edge architecture that made them seem the very newest thing. They began opening for worship in the 12th century, and in the 16th century, Portuguese writer Francisco Álvarez became the first European to see them, and to report back: "I weary of writing more about these buildings, because it seems to me that I shall not be believed if I write more."

Today, the 11 stone churches are all affiliated with the Ethiopian Orthodox religion and Lalibela is the nation's principal pilgrimage destination. Seen on these pages are early morning congregants gathered around Bet Giyorgis, also known now as the Church of St. George, the construction of which was overseen by Lalibela (the man) himself.

UNIVERSAL HISTORY ARCHIVE/GETTY

## IN EVERYONE'S ETERNAL CITY

Except for the fact that they do not and will not share Jerusalem, the three great monotheistic faiths—Judaism, Islam and Christianity—share Jerusalem. It is crucial to all of their histories. It has been battled over, sacked and divided (a condition that continues today).

At right is the Muslim Dome of the Rock atop the Temple Mount in the Old City. If this was the traditional Mount Moriah of the Hebrew Bible, then Isaac was bound here by Abraham. If it was Mount Zion, the original Judaic fort was here. Regardless, the Mount has for millennia been crucially important to the Jewish religion. This is the place Yahweh selected for the residence of the Divine Presence. To go all the way back: Talmudic interpretations have it that the world grew from this spot and that Yahweh gathered dust here to create Adam.

For Christians, 12-year-old Jesus confronted the scholars in the Temple here, and later, near the end of His life, threw out the moneylenders and predicted the Temple's destruction. For centuries it was a place of Christian pilgrimage, and it remains important to those of the Eastern Orthodoxies, who remember that there was a consecrated church here once, and such a place can never be replaced.

Yet now the Mount is dominated by the Dome of the Rock. As for the Islamic side of the story, please turn the page—and enter with us into this grand building.

HANAN ISACHAR/CORBIS

## FROM THIS ROCK

That Islam and Christianity battled over Jerusalem ferociously during the Crusades (and at other times) is well-known history, and that Islam and Judaism are at an impasse that goes deeper than mere loggerheads in Israel in our time is daily news. Nevertheless, many non-Muslims might wonder about this building at this particular site. Isn't Islam about Mecca?

It surely is, but Muslims consider the Mount to be one of the holiest locations in the world: The Noble Sanctuary is the spot from which, in one of the religion's principal miracles (along with Allah's bequeathal of the Koran), Muhammad went from this world to visit heaven, circa 620 (in the 16th-century painting on page 58, a veiled Muhammad ascends on the winged creature Buraq, guided by Jibril and escorted by angels). He had come to Jerusalem, and from Jerusalem his Night Journey began.

While there may be no commonality of purpose or opinion among the three great monotheisms when it comes to Jerusalem, they all share an origin and a great prophet, Abraham—"the father of us all," as Saint Paul (a Jewish convert to Christianity, by the way) put it. Everything was once one, in this place. And everything exploded from here, in a kind of earthbound religious version of the Big Bang. It is still exploding, apparently outward.

Historically, each religion has "owned" this summit at a point in time. At present, atop the Temple Mount sits the Dome of the Rock, and inside is the rock itself, from which Muhammad

FARAH NOSH/GETTY

DAVID LEES/CORBIS

ascended and to which Muslim pilgrims come constantly. (In the photograph at left, women in the shrine in 2004; at right, the focal point.) It is a place of prayer and a historic place of miracles, but also a place of conflict. In 2000 (which, in the passage of time, was not even an eye-blink ago), Ariel Sharon, who hoped to become prime minister of Israel, went to the Temple Mount, hard by the Dome of the Rock and the Al-Aqsa Mosque, and declared that Israel would always control the area. He was accompanied by more than a thousand armed police. One response was Palestinian violence the next day. Sharon won his election. Much more recently, although Israel's chief rabbinate advises Jews not to enter the area, and while Israeli police prohibit visitors who do venture up from the Western Wall from praying, singing or dancing for fear of increasing tensions, more and more Jews see access to the Mount as a basic right and make their way. Not surprisingly, this has led to more and more clashes, some of them bloody, with Muslims who oppose all incursions as sacrilegious. This certainly seems fraught and dangerous now, but remember: In centuries past, temples and churches were torn down here. Perspective helps, but it is not necessarily encouraging.

God's desire for Jerusalem? Different sides have different answers, but let's imagine that God's will is for all the sons and daughters of Abraham to, if not reunite, at least find a familial peace. From the vantage of the present day, that would be a miracle.

## GENTLY ASKING FOR MIRACLES

What is an intercession? It is someone or something entering a situation and effecting change in the process or outcome—interceding for the better, it is to be hoped. Again, to the assassination attempt on John Paul II: The pope felt that Mary had interceded in this event and saved his life.

What goes on daily at the Western Wall in Jerusalem (at right), which is near the Dome of the Rock on the Temple Mount? Hundreds of pilgrims offer their prayers of reverence or gratitude—the Silent Prayer or other prayers. And many insert into the cracks between stones a prayer they think is special, or a prayer accompanied by a request: for help, for strength, for intercession.

The Jewish faith isn't big on miracles that are claimed by others to have occurred in the postbiblical ages, but it sanctions the opinion of the sages that he who prays at the Temple in Jerusalem has prayed as if he had done so before the throne of glory, because the gate of heaven is situated there and it is open to hear prayer. If it is open to hear prayer, then perforce it is open to consider prayer and even to answer prayer. It is good for us to direct this prayer upward from this wall, which once was part of the Temple; the 19th-century scholar Rabbi Jacob Ettlinger said as much: "[S]ince the gate of heaven is near the Western Wall, it is understandable that all Israel's prayers ascend on high there . . . as one of the great ancient kabbalists Rabbi Joseph Gikatilla said, when the Jews send their prayers from the Diaspora in the direction of Jerusalem, from there they ascend by way of the Western Wall."

All of this means not only that prayer is not wasted time, but that intercession is not impossible. Whatever "all Israel's prayers" might be, some of them—big or small—are certainly entreaties.

What is an intercession? If it begins in heaven and helps us here on earth, it is a miracle.

MIRIAM ALSTER/FLASH90/REDUX

RICCARDO BUDINI/DEMOTIX/CORBIS

## MARY REAPPEARS

We have already in these pages dealt a little with Medjugorje—what happened there in the Bosnian mountains, when the events occurred, and what they meant to many of the Catholic faith. The story seemed something of a piece with Lourdes and Fátima: again a child or children, again Mary.

A central difference between the events in what was then Yugoslavia and those that had occurred earlier in Portugal and France is that Medjugorje, for better or worse, was and is a phenomenon of the postmodern age. The word spread faster than it ever could have out of 19th-century Lourdes. Already today, more than 30 million faithful have made their way to Mount Podbrdo—roughly a million per year since the first apparition. (At left we see some of the pilgrims, on July 2, 2012, praying around the statue of the Virgin atop what is now called Apparition Hill).

The media descended quickly and have never really left. The children became and remain celebrities; websites boost them regularly. Some of them lecture around the world. Although the Marian appearances in Lourdes and Fátima ended in the short term, several of the erstwhile children of Medjugorje still receive messages from Mary, and these are quickly posted online. In late September 2013, on Medjugorge.org, followers learned that Mary had communicated these words to Marija Pavlovic, one of the group of visionaires: "Prayer works miracles in you and through you, therefore, little children, may prayer be a joy for you. Then your relationship with life will be deeper and more open and you will comprehend that life is a gift for each of you."

## A PILGRIMAGE'S PROVENANCE

Whistles pierce the marrow-freezing air at two a.m. as hundreds of Indians, dressed in shaggy garb with knit masks, call to one another to begin the final glacial ascent. These are the *ukukus,* young men in mythical half-human, half-bear costumes who are chosen to represent their communities on the pilgrimages.

Qoyllur Rit'i, or Star Snow Festival, is a spiritual and religious festival held each year in the realm of Peru's Machu Picchu. The Catholic Church is fine with this; in fact it claims it in a way, seeing it as a celebration originating in 1780 when a local shepherd boy named Mariano Mayta met a mestizo boy named Manuel in these mountains. Once the two bonded, Mariano's herd prospered. From there, the story gets far more metaphysical: Manuel becomes a bush bearing an image of Christ hanging from it. Then Mariano dies and is buried under a rock, upon which an image of Christ is painted.

Well before the Spanish came to the Andes Mountains of South America and introduced Christianity to the natives, there were celebrations of the stars as part of Incan tradition. The one that accompanied the Southern Hemisphere winter solstice was wonderful. Those rituals did not differ appreciably from the Christian versions to follow, or from what occurs when today's pilgrims, thinking what they will, believing in their own God in their own way, personally sanctioning whatever miracles occurred here, make their arduous way to the summit—faith in hand, God in mind.

## IN SAINT PATRICK'S STEPS

No one is more sentimental than the Irish, and this is not meaning to say several things: that there is anything wrong with sentimentality, that the notion of miracles is inherently sentimental, that religion depends upon sentimentality, or that the Irish are prone to beliefs that others are not prone to. Miracles are spiritual events, and we do not in this book (nor in our thinking) deny spiritual events. But also: The Irish, beyond the sentimentality, are great with a story, and one of their great stories is that of Saint Patrick.

There weren't any snakes in Ireland to drive out. And so this mid-teen slave, who had arrived from Britain in the fifth century, wasn't likely to drive out any snakes—whatever legend may say—or even to stay long. He lived in Ireland for six years, escaped from slavery, returned to his family, became a bishop, returned to Ireland and worked with the people. Patrick was the Irish religious, physical and secular hero the people always dreamed of.

In the photograph on the opposite page, a pilgrim prays on the holy mountain Croagh Patrick in County Mayo. Many like this man go each year and reach the top, some climbing on their bloodied bare feet. It is possible that Patrick himself, who is the patron saint of Ireland, was shod and had an easier climb. But that is the thing about faith: Patrick had had more difficult days earlier, and we all have easier and more difficult days, and sometimes we ask for help. Each year on St. Patrick's Day, we honor the man, and the notion of what he might best represent, in our own way.

COTTON COULSON/NATIONAL GEOGRAPHIC CREATIVE/GETTY

*The caption in the 1958 article, written by editors who were rather miserly with the word* the, *explained this grand overview: "The shrine is seen from spire of its topmost basilica. Pilgrims from the town (background) stream down esplanade, passing River Gave, hospital (upper left), and new underground basilica (upper right). They either mount the curved ramps (center) to churches or pass at left to reach grotto." The "topmost basilica" would have been Alfred Eisenstaedt's goal from the moment he scoped out the place, as Timothy Foote,* LIFE*'s reporter on the story and a man who would go on to edit at both* LIFE *and* Time, *recalled not long ago in the series of reminiscences he offers online in his* Footenotes *pieces: "[Alfred] was enthusiastic and tireless and at 56 wore me out in the pursuit of pictures. He told me that he did 50 pushups every morning before breakfast to keep in shape. I remember him running across a roof and jumping up on a stone parapet that I (six inches taller and 30 years younger) could barely reach. When I'd propose getting back to the hotel, he'd refuse, remarking, 'As my sainted mother used to say, 'Alfred, plenty of time to rest in the grave.'" Just by the way, Eisie lived to be 96.*

ALFRED EISENSTAEDT/LIFE/THE PICTURE COLLECTION

Alfred Eisenstaedt in

# Lourdes

*In 1958 the centenary of Bernadette Soubirous's extraordinary experience in Lourdes was celebrated by* LIFE, *which sent Alfred Eisenstaedt to make pictures of what the magazine called in our original subheadline "a great spectacle of faith."*

WE HAVE ALREADY DEALT IN THESE PAGES with the background of the apparitions at Lourdes, and this now proves a good thing, for it is often fun and even illuminating when revisiting these LIFE stories to see what we wrote at the time. From our introductory text to that 17-page package: "Through the mountain meadows of southern France and from the far corners of Christendom some 8 million pilgrims are journeying to the great Catholic shrine of Lourdes. They have been coming for decades in increasing numbers, but this year their number will exceed all others, for it is the 100th anniversary of the time that young Bernadette knelt in rapture before a low stone grotto and saw visions of 'a girl in white . . . opening her hands just as holy Virgins do.'

"Most of the pilgrims will make the journey as an act of devotion. But many pilgrims are cruelly sick and come to Lourdes filled with sublime hope that the intercession of the Virgin Mary will make them well. They buttress their faith with the thousands of reported cures, as well as the 54 recognized by the Church as miracles. [Editor's note: There have been 15 subsequently.]

"That this renowned shrine should have been born from the visions of an obscure 14-year-old shepherdess seems a miracle in itself. The Virgin's instructions to Bernadette during her 18 apparitions have been meticulously obeyed, as shown on the following pages . . . Today at the grotto the spring which frail Bernadette dug at the Virgin's direction flows to faucets and private tubs where both the sick and healthy by the thousands drink and bathe. 'Tell the priests to build a chapel here,' Bernadette was ordered. Now, directly on top of the grotto, three huge churches tower over a broad esplanade.

"At least 100 million pilgrims have come to Lourdes. The Procession of the Blessed Sacrament [seen on the opposite page] is the time of most fervent hope for miracles and the sick chant, 'Lord, if Thou wilt. Thou canst make me whole. Lord, make me see! Lord, make me hear! Lord, make me walk!' Each night there is a glittering procession by thousands of pilgrims carrying candles [please see pages 48 and 49 of our book], honoring the shepherdess who is now Saint Bernadette and thunderously singing the refrain which is the theme of Lourdes, 'Ave, Ave, Ave, Maria.'"

*In* LIFE *in 1958, there was a main story, and then an adjunct, reported completely by Timothy Foote and shot by Eisenstaedt, focusing on one of the tour groups of ill or infirm that traveled to Lourdes. This one, led by a spiritual adviser accompanied by doctors and nurses and organized by the Catholic Travel Office in Washington, D.C., was called the Pilgrimage of the Sick to Lourdes and included pilgrims, aged from six to 60, who hailed from places as far apart as Baton Rouge and San Francisco, Alaska and Quebec. Their afflictions were many and varied. Donald Spring, 25, of Herndon, Virginia, had, as Foote reported, "spent his lifetime savings to go. Blind for only two months before his pilgrimage, after two earlier unsuccessful brain tumor operations, Donald was not even a Catholic (his people are Baptist and Methodist). He explained, 'I'm open to all religions. I don't expect to get cured, that's for sure. But it's something that I know I'll gain, that I gotta do, coming here. I dunno just what it is.'" The accompanying caption for the photographs on this page explained: "At grotto bath before immersion, Spring stands in the tub steadied by John Hudgson (left), head of the Catholic Travel Office, and a* brancardier, *one of the volunteer crew who assist sick at Lourdes. Immersion in the 50-degree water takes place during recitation of prayer to Virgin inscribed on plaque on wall."*

*Foote later wrote: "There were no miracles" for this group of 40. But: "At the end, Donald Spring declared that he would become a Catholic." Still later, in summation: "The working message of Lourdes was best expressed by 25-year-old Donald Spring, who in the last two years has lost both eyes and has a growing brain tumor which two operations have failed to check and which, barring a miracle, will kill him. 'I hope the others get cured,' he said. 'There's some of 'em is awful bad off.'"*

*Opposite: A photograph from 1958 that never ran and is seen here for the first time, of pilgrims collecting the water that when ingested, they hope, might help them.*

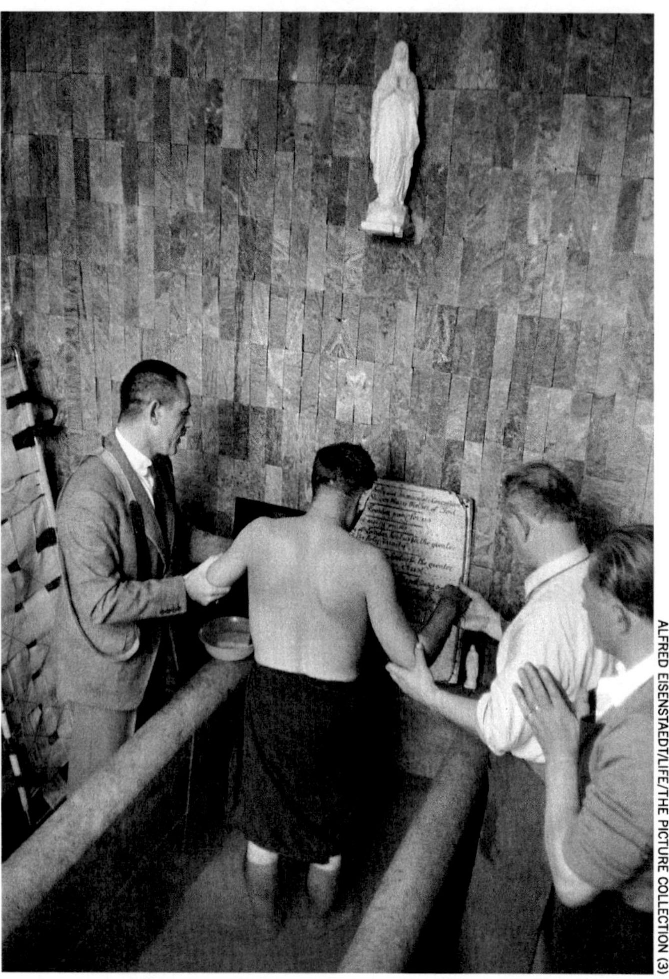

ALFRED EISENSTAEDT/LIFE/THE PICTURE COLLECTION (3)

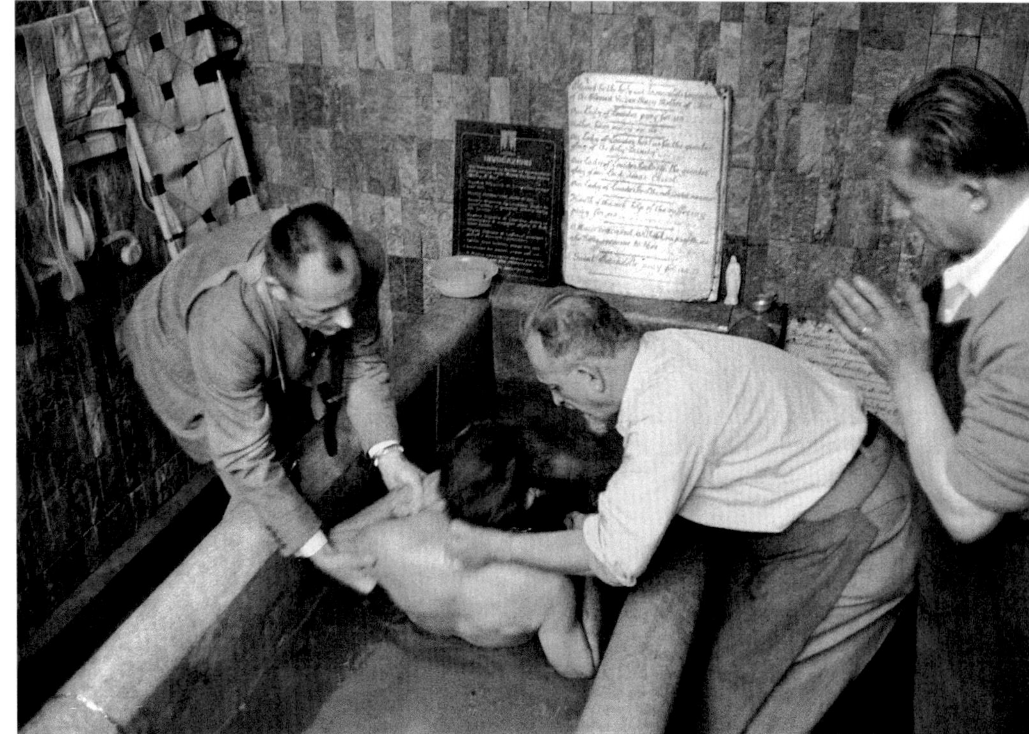

*These are two more photographs from our archives seen here for the first time, although their story was told in captions for other pictures. Below, we see people with afflictions making their way to Mass, and at right, we see a blessing being bestowed upon them. "Mass for sick is held daily at 7:30 a.m. in front of grotto. The sick are arranged in ranks on wheeled litters which have canvas hoods to keep off rain or sun. Well pilgrims are kept back along the bank of the Gave River," wrote* LIFE's *editors at the time. "Blessing on sick during Procession of Blessed Sacrament is spiritual high point of day. Priest, passing down line of litters, makes sign of the Cross with Host which is contained in monstrance protected by umbrella."*

*As emotional as the message of these photographs obviously is, this wasn't a particularly taxing story for* LIFE *photographer Eisenstaedt or reporter Foote. But Eisie was Jewish German by birth and had fled his homeland for America, and there was this, as Foote has recently remembered in his* Footenotes *postings: "When we got to Lourdes, the crowds of sick pilgrims and the constant en bloc praying ('*Je vous salue Marie, pleine de grace'*) and the sheer commerce did not make Alfred uneasy . . .*

*"We visited the man who had the candle concession for Bernadette's grotto.*

ALFRED EISENSTAEDT/LIFE/THE PICTURE COLLECTION (2)

*His largest candle was four feet tall and 12 inches in diameter. We visited young Dr. Soubirous, a prosperous descendant of the saint's once-impoverished family. Pilgrims and tourists, he complained, often made a medical appointment, but clearly with miraculous cures in mind; once in his office, they'd ask to touch him. He seemed mortally offended, just at the recollection:* 'C'est du fétishisme ça!' *he exclaimed.*

*"Only once did Alfred offer a real comment on what we saw and heard going on around us. This occurred when we found ourselves one morning at breakfast in the Golgotha Hotel (no less) with a group of German pilgrims. Alfred sat silent throughout the meal, listening intently. But when we went up to the room to collect our gear for the day's shooting, he had an urgent need to talk. 'I know them all,' he said. 'All of them around the table.' And with devastating precision he went round the table, saying how this one or that one would have behaved in Germany in the early 1930s. He made delicate distinctions in predicting their behavior. The only one I remember applied to a jolly-looking woman at the far end of the table. 'She would be one to wring her hands and say, "Oh, it's terrible what's happening." And then go down and inform on you.'"*

*Lourdes has stirred all feelings since 1858, and ever will.*

# The Miracles of the Saints

*What is a saint? There is no answer to that question that would be (or should be) accepted universally. In colloquial conversation, a saint is the guy or gal in the next cubicle who brings doughnuts on Friday. Or he is the tight end who gives himself up on the big block to spring the glorified running back. Or she is the understudy who practices her steps and cues, never daring to hope the star gets hurt but, rather, supporting her, actually helping her improve. None of these claims to sainthood is wrong: There are saintly folk among us, exemplars—our thousand points of light. Do we presume God doesn't see them as saints? That would be a large presumption, certainly. But having said all that, the Roman Catholic Church has a long practice of canonizing, which is to say authorizing, its saints, and while the criteria were once rather loose—based, in many cases, as much on notoriety, legend or administrative position (lots of popes) as on transcendent holiness—in our day there are firm rules. There must be two miracles credited: posthumous intercessions by the late candidate, who, it is deemed, has affected life on earth from a heavenly situation. There must be forceful arguments made on behalf of the candidate. It is very much like the action in a human court of law, which serves to confuse what we are talking about. This is not, after all, about considering a petitioner or a plaintiff. This is about a possible saint. On the following pages, we consider some of those who are now officially recognized saints. What they indisputably share: Each has an astonishing story.*

GABRIEL BOUYS/AFP/GETTY

The two newest Roman Catholic saints, canonized by Pope Francis on April 27, 2014, were exceptional men: Pope John XXIII, who launched the revivifying Vatican II conference in the 1960s, and Pope John Paul II (seen here during a Mass of Beatification for Anton Martin Slomsek on September 19, 1999), who as a whip-smart young cardinal from Poland named Karol Wojtyla saw his star rise in the Church through his work at Vatican II. We will return to John Paul a few pages on.

RICHARD T. NOWITZ

## JOSEPH

Recognized by all of us today to have been the husband of Mary, he isn't even mentioned in all of the four New Testament Gospels. Matthew and Luke have it that Mary was engaged to Joseph before Jesus's birth, but if we want to know Saint Joseph as a human being, we have to rely solely on Matthew's account. His narrative of Jesus's infancy is written largely from Joseph's point of view, in fact. Obviously the man wrestles with how to deal with his fiancée's unexpected pregnancy; in this, and in later travails, particularly threats against his son, he is helped by counseling angels.

Joseph, in Matthew, has four dreams in which he is instructed by God's agents. In his first dream, an angel tells the betrothed Joseph that, indeed, Mary is with child, but that conception was by the Holy Spirit. Joseph is informed that she will bear a son, to be named Jesus, and that this boy will be extraordinary in the world. In fact, He is being sent to save humanity from its sinfulness. Joseph should, therefore, marry Mary. Everything is understood.

In Joseph's second dream, depicted at left in *Rest on the Flight into Egypt (Joseph's Dream),* by Lambert Krahe, an angel warns Joseph that home is becoming a dangerous place—Herod is looking to find and kill Jesus—and tells him to take Mary and Jesus to Egypt. Further instructions will follow. In Joseph's third dream, an angel instructs him to return to Israel. He learns that Herod is dead but hears that Herod's son now reigns, and he doesn't know where to go. In a fourth dream, a new voice, perhaps that of God Himself, addresses Joseph, and he settles in the Galilean backwater of Nazareth, where he sets up as a carpenter.

That, according to Matthew, is why we have Jesus of Nazareth, not of Bethlehem or some other place.

There are no further miracles involving Saint Joseph—in fact, there is no further mention of him at all after Jesus's childhood. Mary is alone at Cana with Jesus; she is with her women friends at the crucifixion. It is assumed she was long a widow. We cannot be sure.

## JOHN THE BAPTIST

He was a wild character—charismatic; in an evocative modern term, *out there.* He came from a line of priests, but by young adulthood he had become an ascetic subsisting on insects and honey, wearing the robe and belt of a prophet, wandering in the Judaean wilderness. To those who would listen, and increasing numbers did, he said that the Abrahamic heritage was insufficient, that God had brought Israel out of Egypt and across the Jordan River to create a new people, that God surely expected things of these people. Baptism in the Jordan (above, the calm waters near Tiberias, where pilgrims still come for baptism) could signal repentance, said John. He wasn't putting forward a new religion. In fact he was saying that religion alone is not God. God is justice, and radical repentance can show us all the way. John proclaimed that in anticipation of the coming judgment, we should cleanse ourselves of sin right now and behave as if the reckoning were five minutes away.

As John the Baptist became more famous (and so influential that the authorities would find it necessary to bring him in and, subsequently, have him beheaded), he famously claimed that he was not "the one," that someone would come after him whose bootstraps he himself, John, was not worthy to tie. Jesus was baptized by John in the Jordan River. The message of the two men was in sync then, and it still is.

SCALA/ART RESOURCE, NY

## THOMAS, AND THOMAS

The appellation "Saint" applies to many men named John—the evangelist, the Baptist, John of the Cross . . . So, too, with Thomas: There are quite a few with this name, and any of their stories is worth recounting. Here, we speak of two: Thomas Aquinas and Thomas the Apostle.

The 13th-century Dominican friar Thomas of Aquino (in present-day Italy) is regarded, even all these centuries later, as perhaps the Church's greatest-ever philosopher and theologian. His philosophy, Thomism, sought to reconcile, really for the first time with any seriousness, religious thinking and natural reason. For his quarrelsomeness (above, confounding the heretics, in a 15th-century fresco by Filippino Lippi), he was reprimanded by the bishop of Paris at one point, but Thomas would be the immortal one. In the 14th century, when his sainthood was being debated, the question was asked, Where are the miracles? To which one cardinal answered brilliantly: "There are as many miracles [in his life] as articles."

Much earlier, another Thomas was one of Christ's apostles. He is named in all lists of the 12 but is a player only in the Gospel of John, in which his doubting of Jesus's divinity after the Resurrection leads to the dramatic scene in which Thomas says he won't believe until he places his hand in the wound. It was later said of him (not in the New Testament) that he was so convinced, he evangelized as far afield as India. At right: A small bone in this glass case in India is said to be a section of his forearm.

LYNN JOHNSON/NATIONAL GEOGRAPHIC CREATIVE

ERICH LESSING/ART RESOURCE, NY



More than God, more than Jesus, Mary is the great intercessor—which is to say, the ultimate miracle worker. That many of us feel a need for Mary, the Blessed Mother, the Mother of Jesus, is indisputable. Why we need Mary, and what we hope to receive from Mary—these are more involved considerations. "We live in a society where iron and cement triumph," the late Father Stefano de Fiores, a former professor of Historical Mariology at the Pontifical Gregorian University in Rome, once told LIFE. "Mary is an irreproachable figure esthetically, and responds to two great needs in such a society. For belonging. And for tenderness."

Can it possibly be as simple at that? For some, it can be. Mary soothes, and that is enough. For others, the issue of Mary—the concept of Mary, the person who was Mary, the presence of Mary today—is infinitely more complex.

The complexity extends from the simplicity: Hers is a very scant biography. The Mary of the New Testament is the mother of Jesus, more or less full stop. She is mentioned (and always with respect) more often in the Koran than she is in the Bible. Her life was defined by two great miracles, neither of which she purposely wrought: the Immaculate Conception and her Assumption into heaven (seen at left in a depiction from the altarpiece of the St. Sulpice church in Paris; below is the Tomb of the Virgin Mary beneath the Church of the Assumption in Jerusalem). "You could copy on an eight-and-a-half-by-eleven sheet everything there is about Mary in the New Testament," the late Jaroslav Pelikan, a professor at Yale and author of *Mary Through the Centuries,* told LIFE. "To get from such skimpy evidence to what she has become is an astonishing example of how an idea can develop out of small beginnings."

But it is the elemental idea, is it not? "Belonging," as Father de Fiores said. "Tenderness."

Jesus needed—and we all need—a mother.

RICHARD T. NOWITZ/CORBIS

SUMMERFIELD PRESS/CORBIS

ROBERTO NISTRI/ALAMY

## FRANCIS

Yes, there are more than a couple of Saint Francises, too, and if the current pope keeps steaming along as he has been, there may be another, one day. We are referring here to Saint Francis of Assisi, seen above, left, in a 15th-century painting by Francesco Francia (at right is the St. Francis of Assisi hermitage in Rieti, Lazio, Italy).

He is one of the most beloved religious figures in human history. His story has it all: sin, repentance, animals. This is the man who is said to have invented the Christmas crèche to commemorate the Nativity.

He was born in the late 12th century in Italy to luxurious circumstances, in which he reveled. He drank, he debauched, he fought—sometimes officially, as a soldier. After the war, however, something called him back home to Assisi, and whatever epiphany he experienced, it would prove enduring. Suddenly the high life was not for him. He traveled to Rome, and everything that he had been came undone. He helped the beggars at St. Peter's Basilica in their entreaties; he listed toward a life of poverty himself; he became an ascetic. He returned to Assisi a thoroughly changed man and gained adherents. His love was boundless and ecumenical—more so than that of the male-dominated Church itself. He founded the Order of Brothers and Sisters of Penance and also the Order of the Poor Clares.

His legacies are many, and strong. Most predominantly, there are the Franciscans within the Roman Catholic Church: clerics dedicated to his principles who try to live as Francis did. The current pontiff is a Jesuit, yet he disclosed when choosing his papal name that he hoped to honor Francis of Assisi. Francis is the patron saint not only of animals—when your dog or cat or goldfish gets blessed each year in the church parking lot, Francis is evoked—but also of the environment. He is and always will be Francis, sine qua non.

SCALA/ART RESOURCE, NY

GIANNI DAGLI ORTI/THE ART ARCHIVE/ART RESOURCE, NY

## GEORGE

Most of the saints in this chapter are here for every good reason: They are, like Francis or Catherine on these two pages, among the very best expressions of humanity that our meager human condition can offer. A couple of them, however, we freely admit, are here because anyone might ask, "Hey, what about . . . ?" They illustrate the depth and breadth of our belief in miracles, perhaps, and so the validity of their inclusion in a book such as this is arguable. But the counterargument to whether that space could be better used on a more illustrious saint can (and probably should) be made as well. And yet . . . Joseph of Cupertino, whom you will meet on the very next page, could fly, and George killed a dragon. Fun stuff. We're keeping them in.

George was a different kind of saint for reasons other than his dragon-killing (seen above, in a 19th-century painting by Eugene Delacroix). For one thing, he was born, circa 280, to a Greek Christian noble family in Cappadocia and his fame transcends even Christendom; he is one of the precious few "official" saints with a strong historical personality in Islam as well. He apparently had lost both his parents by the time he was an adolescent. His family's heritage was military, and George became an officer in the Roman army, ascending to be the emperor's aide. After centuries of doubt as to whether Saint George, who is the patron saint of England, ever really walked the earth, his historic existence has been generally conceded, but we should maybe leave the factual record at what we have just written.

The legend is more vibrant. In the year 302, the emperor Diocletian ordered that all Christian soldiers be arrested. With George, this presented a problem: Diocletian valued him greatly and tried vigorously to convert him, but George was resolute in his faith and vowed allegiance to Jesus Christ, refuting all Roman gods. He was tortured, then martyred.

Oh, yes: He had slain a dragon earlier, when proving himself to the emperor.

## CATHERINE

Francis of Assisi is posthumously busy as a patron saint: He is a friend of animals and the environment, and he is also one of two patron saints of Italy. The other is Catherine of Siena, and he couldn't be in better company.

She was, like Thomas Aquinas, a thinker, a philosopher. She stands as an early and critically important representative of a strain of Christian worship that has, interestingly and perhaps paradoxically, grown ever more intriguing and influential in our scientific age: mysticism. In 1970 she was proclaimed a Doctor of the Church by Pope Paul VI and in 1999 was named one of the six patron saints of Europe by Pope John Paul II, who often wrote respectfully of Catherine and other mystics. In mysticism lie miracles, and Catholicism has certainly never shied from the miraculous.

Caterina di Giacomo di Benincasa was born on March 25, 1347, during the plague, her mother's 23rd child. She lived, and was nicknamed "Euphrosyne"—Greek for "Joy." She had her first vision when still a little girl; it was not of Mary but of Jesus, seated with the apostles Peter, Paul and John. At seven years old she promised to dedicate herself to God. As a teenager, she recoiled at her mother's idea of an arranged marriage to the widower of one of her sisters and developed a strategy that would serve her (and many teenagers in the centuries to come): "Build a cell inside your mind, from which you can never flee." Catherine, vigorously imaginative and energetically devout, created an inner life in which her father was a Christ figure, her mother was a version of Mary, and her brothers were apostles. When she was 21, she experienced what she later wrote was a mystical marriage with Jesus. This union has been interpreted often in art. (Above: *The Mystic Marriage of Saint Catherine of Siena before Saint Sebastian,* by Antonio da Correggio, circa 1527.)

She traveled throughout Italy, gaining followers and fame. She wrote to public figures, including the pope, and her opinions were influential. She tried to broker a peace between Florence and Rome (Italy was divided into city-states at that time); she worked with Pope Urban VI to heal the Western Schism. But she took to rigorous fasting, nourished only by the Host of Holy Communion, and died at 33 in 1380.

RMN-GRAND PALAIS/ART RESOURCE, NY

## JOAN

You know her as Joan of Arc (above: *Joan of Arc Kissing the Sword of Deliverance,* by Dante Gabriel Rossetti). The French and the Joan cognoscenti also know her as the Maid of Orléans, the city that would be the site of her great triumph. Because the details of her life and exploits were of the long-ago Middle Ages, they are sketchy in places, but they are nonetheless riveting—at least as we understand and believe them.

She was born to peasant stock in the Champagne province in northeastern France in 1412. Her father, Jacques d'Arc, worked a small farm. Although some traditions hold otherwise, Joan was not a shepherdess or milker of cows. She was an uncommonly pious girl and was observed kneeling in church, praying for the poor. Not many years later, at her trial, prosecutors tried to make her seem a superstitious and spooky figure by saying that she had danced around the Fairy Tree with other children. Maybe she had, and so be it.

Joan's hometown was loyal to Charles VII, the French king, while the opposing Burgundians saw the future in the English. In the summer of 1425, at age 13, she began to hear voices, which were later accompanied by blazes of light and which she later identified as belonging to Saint Michael, Saint Margaret and Saint Catherine. Following her call, she became a soldier, a leader and the champion of great French victories, including that at Orléans. When she was captured and put on trial for insubordination and heterodoxy, Joan told her judges: "I saw [the saints] with these very eyes, as well as I see you." She was burned at the stake but was later exonerated and canonized.

## JOSEPH OF CUPERTINO

The Middle Ages ran to nearly the end of the 15th century, say the history books. But medieval thinking did not die out overnight, and here we have a saint, born in 1603, whose renown rests on one particular talent: his ability to fly (below, in an 18th-century painting by Ludovico Mazzanti).

Giuseppe Maria Desa was born in a stable in the village of Cupertino, which was then in the kingdom of Naples, part of today's Italy. Why in a stable can only be speculated (perhaps there was no room at the inn). But it is known that his father had died before Giuseppe's birth, and the family home had been seized to repay some of the many debts owed by the senior Desa.

Joseph was not an easy child for his mother or others to deal with. As a scholar, he was lacking—frankly, he was considered a dunce—and he was unruly to boot. And he had a temper. On top of this, he behaved abnormally, talking of ecstatic visions.

Apprenticed to a shoemaker, Joseph wasn't content. He felt the religious life might be his future and applied to the Conventual Franciscan friars. They turned him down due to his lack of schooling. He went to the Capuchin friars in Martino and they accepted him as a lay brother. But his ecstasies soon proved too much for them, and he was out again. Back home, he was ostracized, and he went knocking once more on the door of the Franciscans. This time, they said he could work in the stables. It was fine with Joseph, and his devotion to God only increased now that he was in the friary. The priests, over time, were impressed, and in 1628, at not quite 25 years of age, Joseph was ordained.

In the next years, the ecstasies increased in frequency and fervor. Reports leaked out that he was levitating during Mass—ultimately he "flew" more than 100 times, it was said, once in front of the pope—and as witchcraft was then a subject of the Inquisition, he was investigated. He was allowed to return to the supervision of the Conventuals and died in their community in 1663. Joseph was beatified and canonized a century later, and his fame is secure: He is the flying priest and the patron saint of, among other groups, air travelers and astronauts.

FORTEAN/TOPFOTO/THE IMAGE WORKS

ALBUM/ART RESOURCE, NY

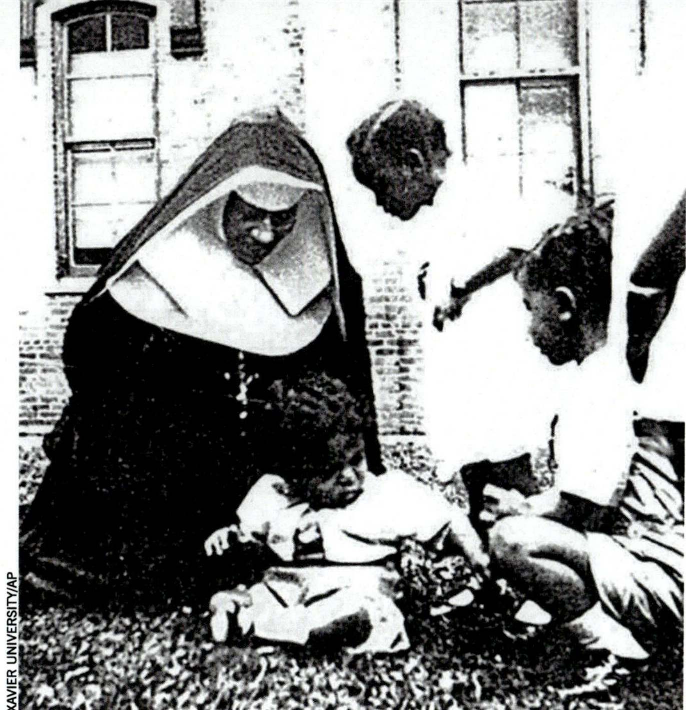
XAVIER UNIVERSITY/AP

## IGNATIUS

Nothing as large and global and old as the Roman Catholic Church would find itself, these many centuries on, without factions in its ranks taking things to, if not another level, at least a somewhat different level. The Society of Jesus, popularly known as the Jesuits, has, since its beginning in 1539, been one such faction. Its founder and first "Superior General" was a knight from a Basque noble family in Spain, a priest named Ignatius of Loyola. Born in 1491, injured in battle in 1521, he found himself suddenly called to God and he determined to emulate holy men such as Francis of Assisi. He was steadfastly loyal to his Church and his pope, but he had many ideas and—after being blessed with a vision of the Virgin Mary and the infant Jesus—began meditating and praying many times a day, on some days for most of his waking hours, developing his Spiritual Exercises. These would be the underpinnings of the Jesuits: a strain of Catholicism that asked much in terms of devotion, penance, ecumenical outreach, learning and self-examination. (Above: Ignatius presents the Jesuit company's rules to Pope Paul III, as depicted in a stained-glass window in his basilica in Gúipuzcoa, Spain.)

He started down his steadfast path with six buddies, none of whom were priests, at university in Paris in 1534. They shared vows with one another, and when his Society began serving the pope as missionaries, the attraction of Ignatius's message was abundantly clear. He was eloquent and a born leader; as a spiritual director he was without peer. He was also steadfastly Catholic and a vigorous opponent of the Protestant Reformation.

The Jesuits are, of course, a mighty faction within the Catholic Church today; Pope Francis is a Jesuit. Many of the world's great universities—in the United States alone: Boston College, Georgetown, Holy Cross, Fordham, not to mention a handful of Loyolas, and on and on—are Jesuit. And Ignatius's meditations and prayers, compiled between 1522 and 1541 with the intention that they could fill the mind of a serious person for a month, then could be repeated, are still in use in the 21st century—in use, and as useful as ever.

## KATHARINE DREXEL

There is a handsome church in New Hampshire not far from Lake Winnipesaukee in the semirural heart of the state. It is filled every Sunday. In winter, there are skiers who are headed for Gunstock populating the early-morning Masses, and in summer there are vacationers and weekenders swelling the congregation's ranks. In foliage season, standees are three rows deep. But even in mud season, when the locals are left on their own, the church is vibrant: American Catholicism at its best, applauding the energetic choir, praying for the parish's children who are fighting wars abroad. The parish is one of more than a dozen in the United States named for Katharine Drexel (above, in the 1920s), who had nothing at all to do with Alton, New Hampshire. Yet the thoughtful people of this congregation could not be more proud.

Why? Who was Katharine Drexel?

She was born in Philadelphia in 1858, became a nun in 1891 and died in 1955. In November 1988, she was beatified by John Paul II, who hailed the former American heiress for devoting her life and fortune to fighting "the devastating effects of racism." On October 1, 2000, the blessed Mother was canonized.

Digging deeper, we find a most special human being.

Her father, an investment banker, was as rich as Croesus; her uncle founded and funded Drexel University. She, like her sisters, was a Main Line debutante. But on a family trip to the West, she witnessed the plight of destitute Native Americans, and helping them and equally beleaguered African Americans became her mission. MISS DREXEL ENTERS A CATHOLIC CONVENT, read the banner headline in Philadelphia's *Public Ledger,* GIVES UP SEVEN MILLION. Much of her share of the family fortune would go to charitable causes, including the establishment of several schools.

Katharine Drexel as a candidate for sainthood was credited with miracles, but the true miracle here is that God finds such people as Thomas Aquinas and Katharine Drexel and guides them to the way. It happens more often than we acknowledge. In each case: a subtle miracle.

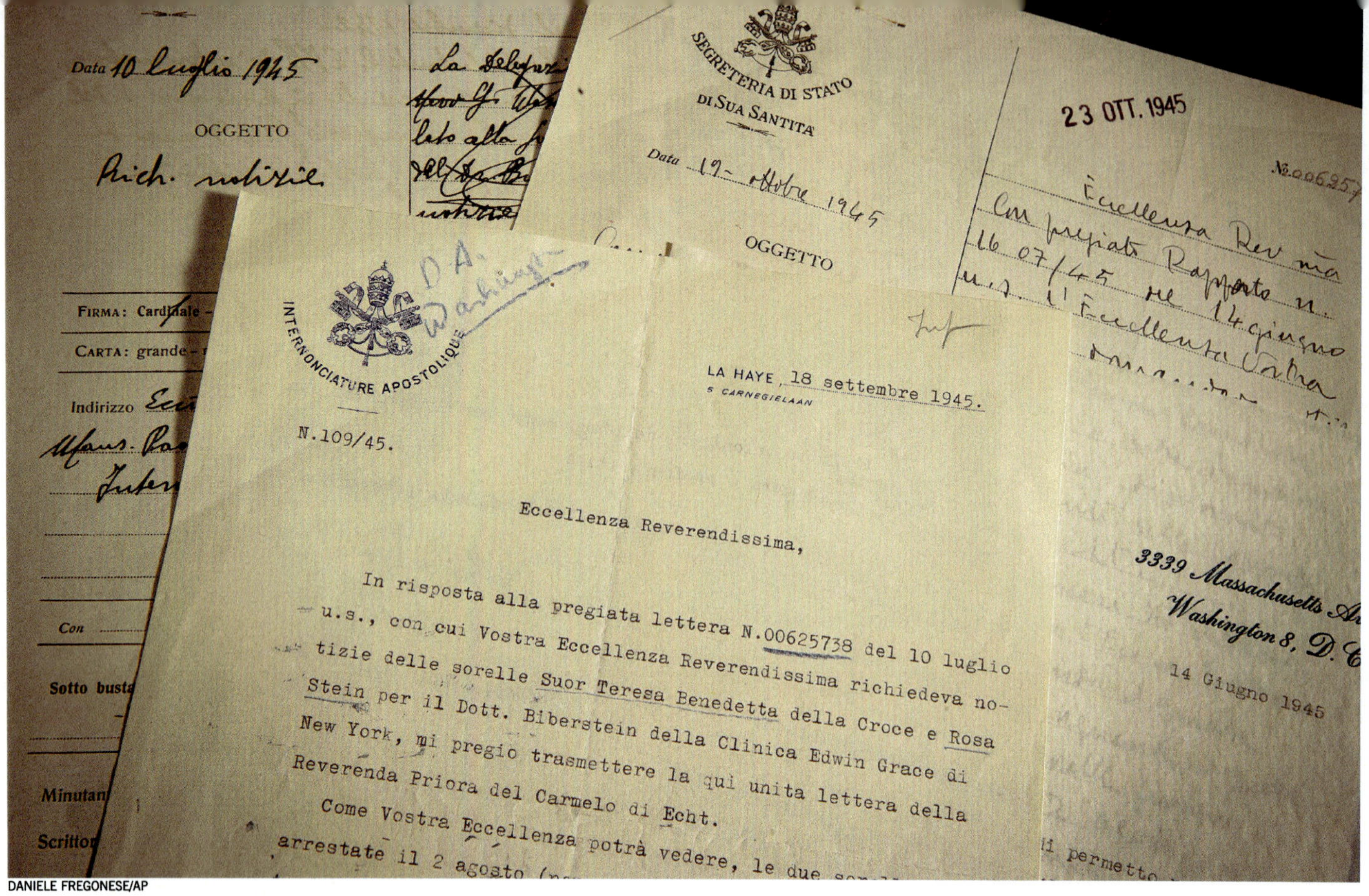

Data 10 luglio 1945
OGGETTO
FIRMA: Cardinale
CARTA: grande
Indirizzo
Con
Sotto busta
Minutan
Scrittor
SEGRETERIA DI STATO DI SUA SANTITÀ
Data 19 ottobre 1945
OGGETTO
23 OTT. 1945
INTERNONCIATURE APOSTOLIQUE
N.109/45.
LA HAYE, 18 settembre 1945.
5 CARNEGIELAAN
Eccellenza Reverendissima,
In risposta alla pregiata lettera N.00625738 del 10 luglio
u.s., con cui Vostra Eccellenza Reverendissima richiedeva no-
tizie delle sorelle Suor Teresa Benedetta della Croce e Rosa
Stein per il Dott. Biberstein della Clinica Edwin Grace di
New York, mi pregio trasmettere la qui unita lettera della
Reverenda Priora del Carmelo di Echt.
Come Vostra Eccellenza potrà vedere, le due
arrestate il 2 agosto
3339 Massachusetts Av
Washington 8, D. C.
14 Giugno 1945

DANIELE FREGONESE/AP

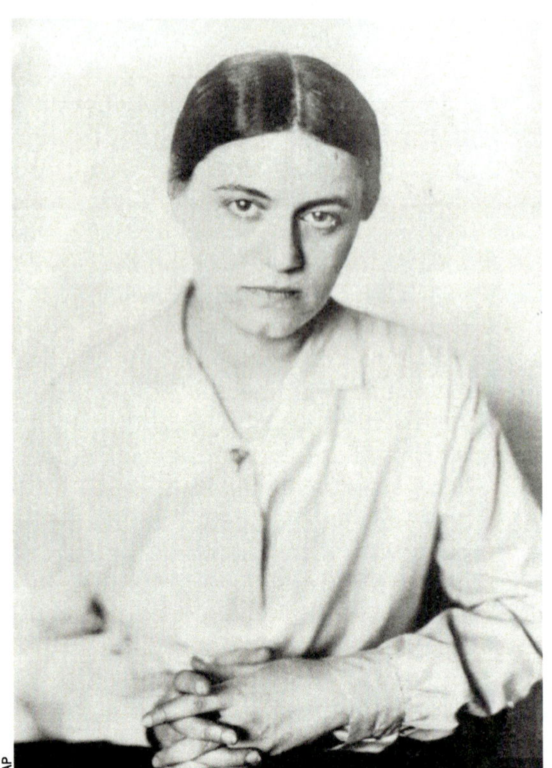

AP

## EDITH STEIN

In 1891 she was born into a German Jewish family on Yom Kippur, the holiest day in the Hebrew year; as a girl she was inspired by her mother's devoutness. But her parents also encouraged intellectual pursuits, and Edith began the questioning and philosophizing that would mark her life. By her teens she was an atheist; then as a young woman she read a biography of the mystic Saint Teresa of Ávila and was greatly influenced. She was baptized a Catholic in 1922. She became a nun, and not a quiet one. "As a child of the Jewish people who, by the grace of God, for the past 11 years has also been a child of the Catholic Church, I dare to speak to the Father of Christianity about that which oppresses millions of Germans," she wrote to Pope Pius XI in 1933, not long before receiving her holy orders. "For weeks we have seen deeds perpetrated in Germany which mock any sense of justice and humanity, not to mention love of neighbor. For years the leaders of National Socialism have been preaching hatred of the Jews . . . But the responsibility must fall, after all, on those who brought them to this point and it also falls on those who keep silent in the face of such happenings. Everything that happened and continues to happen on a daily basis originates with a government that calls itself 'Christian.' For weeks not only Jews but also thousands of faithful Catholics in Germany, and, I believe, all over the world, have been waiting and hoping for the Church of Christ to raise its voice to put a stop to this abuse of Christ's name."

Eventually relocated to the Netherlands for their protection, Edith and her sister Rosa, who had also converted, were arrested there after the Nazis overran Holland. They were sent to Auschwitz in Poland, where they died in the gas chamber. (Above is a letter from the Vatican Secret Archives detailing the Steins' fate.) Edith was canonized by the Polish Pope John Paul II in 1998 in Rome. Some Jews have protested that the Catholic Church is appropriating the legacy of a woman who died because she was Jewish. The Church has answered that in part Sister Teresa Benedicta of the Cross was killed because she was in opposition to Hitler's evil, and thus was a true martyr.

## PADRE PIO

Cults sometimes arise within the Church; it can be said that such men as Thomas Aquinas or Ignatius of Loyola, with their great charisma and original thinking, became cult leaders. In the 20th century, a large cult formed around the former Francesco Forgione, who gained fame as the Italian Capuchin priest known as Padre Pio (right, celebrating Mass). Even as he built up his army of adherents, he was investigated, censured and rehabilitated by Rome, and finally was canonized a saint by Pope John Paul II in 2002.

Why was he a controversial figure? It certainly wasn't for his teachings, which were simple and direct. He urged twice daily meditation—once in the morning to prepare for the day, once in the evening in order to reflect—and weekly confession. His motto was "Pray, Hope, and Don't Worry." But since an early age he was given to visions and ecstasies, and some of his fellow young friars and others later testified to all manner of strange behavior, including levitation. Pio was constantly physically and psychologically afflicted, and the Vatican had its senior exorcist look into the matter. And then there were the stigmata: mysterious bleedings of the hands, feet and side said to be in emulation of Christ's wounds on the cross. Some fellow clergy were drawn to him, others repulsed, one calling him "an ignorant and self-mutilating psychopath." He was banned from exercising his priestly duties for a short term, then reinstated by Pope Pius XI, who said, "I have not been badly disposed toward Padre Pio, but I have been badly informed." Padre Pio died in 1968 at age 81.

KEYSTONE/GETTY

VIVIANE RIVIÈRE/ROGER-VIOLLET/THE IMAGE WORKS

## MAXIMILIAN KOLBE

He too, like Edith and Rosa Stein, died in the Nazi concentration camp at Auschwitz. Upon his canonization in 1982, Kolbe was described by Pope John Paul II as the "patron saint of our difficult century."

He was, like the pope, Polish, and like the pope he was uncommonly dedicated to Mary. Born in 1894, he was just a boy when one night the Virgin "came to me holding two crowns, one white, the other red. She asked if I was willing to accept either of these crowns. The white one meant that I should persevere in purity, and the red that I should become a martyr. I said that I would accept them both."

Kolbe was ordained a priest in 1918. He was a vigorous evangelist in the years prior to World War II, then did quieter work when the Nazis rolled into Poland, sheltering refugees, among them 2,000 Jews. He was found out and arrested on February 17, 1941; soon he was prisoner No. 16670 at Auschwitz. In July 1941, a prisoner escaped and the deputy camp commander ordered 10 men be starved to death to set an example. When one of those selected yelled, "My wife! My children!" Kolbe volunteered to die in his stead. He celebrated Mass daily and sang Marian hymns to his fellow prisoners as they slowly died in their shared bunker during the next two weeks. The guards tired of Kolbe's perseverance and injected him with lethal carbolic acid. He was cremated on August 15, the Feast of the Assumption of Mary.

BETTMANN/CORBIS

## DOROTHY DAY

On the last two pages of this chapter, we present a fairly recent saint and two people who are at different stages of the sainthood process. Each of these three stories is fascinating and worth knowing.

Born in Brooklyn in 1897, Dorothy Day was a journalist and activist (she didn't mind the term *anarchist*) whose Catholicism (she was a convert) informed her work. As this photograph, in which she is standing between Rose Cohn and Charlotte Margolies during a stay-out-of–World War I event, implies, Day was a pacifist. She was also a progressive, and in the 1930s teamed with the French immigrant Peter Maurin, a man inspired by the life of Francis of Assisi, to found the Catholic Worker Movement, which continues to help the poor and homeless today.

But many people in our world do good work. Why would anyone call this particular woman saintly in a formal sense?

It is because it seems that God—or some metaphysicial power—called to her; there was an awakening. Her parents, Protestants, weren't particularly religious, but young Dorothy enjoyed Bible stories. Still, as a young woman she lived a bohemian life: a brief marriage, a love affair, an abortion, the birth of a daughter. On her travels, she had bought a rosary, and now she started to think more deeply about what life might truly mean. One day in New York, she struck up a conversation with a nun, who helped her get her daughter baptized, then helped engineer Dorothy's own conversion.

Day found Catholicism's social teachings regarding the poor a perfect match for her already formed political viewpoint. Through *The Catholic Worker* periodical and the organization's support houses and communal farms (very much needed during the Great Depression in the United States), she and Maurin reached out and effected real change. They also influenced attitudes; they changed some minds. Day tried to cause what she called "a revolution of the heart," and in individual cases, inspired by God, she succeeded.

RAGHU RAI/MAGNUM (2)

ANDREAS SOLARO/AFP/GETTY

## TERESA AND JOHN PAUL

There is a very unofficial term in Rome: the *fast track* to sainthood. Not long after Mother Teresa of Calcutta died in 1997, she was beatified by Pope John Paul II and appeared poised to be a record-breaker. But once John Paul himself was made a saint by Pope Francis in the spring of 2014, Teresa was beaten to the firmament by her patron. Not, of course, that there's a competition.

Agnes Gonxha Bojaxhiu, the girl who would grow up to become Mother Teresa, was born in 1910 in what is now Macedonia. By age 12 she had determined to devote herself to the service of God, and at 18 she left home to join the Sisters of Loreto. Among other activities, this order taught children in India, and Teresa arrived in that country in 1929. She worked at a convent school in Calcutta (now called Kolkata); in 1946 she experienced a "call within a call" to work directly with the poor. She founded the Missionaries of Charity in Calcutta in 1950. In something of a miracle, the Missionaries eventually expanded into more than 100 countries; it was operating some 600 missions at the time of Teresa's death. In December 2015, it was announced that Mother Teresa was expected to be made a saint in the fall of 2016.

The Reverend Billy Graham was forthright about John Paul II when he once told LIFE's readers: "Few individuals have had a greater impact—not just religiously but socially and morally—on the modern world." Just so: The great events of the 20th century influenced Karol Wojtyla's extraordinary life, and as pope he influenced events in turn. In Nazi-occupied Poland, Wojtyla studied for the priesthood at a clandestine seminary in Krakow, then, after the war, rose in the Church, eventually and stunningly becoming the first non-Italian pope in more than four centuries. As pontiff he quickly proved an indomitable force. Working behind the scenes with other world leaders, he played a crucial role in the fall of godless communism. Traveling more miles than all previous popes combined, he was his church's greatest evangelist since Saint Paul. Like Dorothy Day, he was a holy person and a political one—and now he is a saint.

Counterclockwise from top: Teresa in 1979; with John Paul during his visit to her mission in 1986; then the Vatican dossier detailing the late pope's "life, virtues and reputation for saintliness."

# Is This Jesus?

*We know this to be true: The so-called Shroud of Turin is among the most examined artifacts in human history—it perhaps tops them all. This is fitting. The burial cloth of Jesus, one of mankind's most famous figures, deserves such attention. But is it actually Jesus's shroud? Ah, there's the rub. Even in the 21st century, with scientists and theologians pontificating with absolute certainty on both sides of the question, and with us knowing more about the shroud than we ever have, we don't have proof positive. Which puts the shroud into the category of faith and belief, which is, after all, where miracles reside.*

ROGER ARCHIBALD/AURORA

## APPARENTLY LOST AND SUDDENLY FOUND

In the 15th-century painting by Caspar Isenmann at right, which is a detail from the high altar of St. Martin's Church in Colmar, France, Christ has been taken down from the cross and is laid upon a burial sheath, as was customary. The Gospel of John records that a cloth was used to cover Christ's head, while strips of linen were placed upon the body. (But remember: John's is only one of four authorized Gospels.) The El Greco painting below is of Saint Veronica, who wiped Christ's face while He was on His way to Calvary. Maybe this is meant to represent the cloth she used, or maybe it's the cloth referred to in John. We could wear out the word *maybe* in this account, and so we will now refrain.

Here are the basics: In Turin, Italy, there resides, in the Cathedral of San Giovanni Battista, the Holy Shroud: a 14-foot-three-inch-long piece of linen that seems to bear the bloodstains and body image of a crucified man of reasonable height. Was this the cloth once draped over the crucified Christ? That question has been the fundamental one for more than six centuries, ever since the shroud emerged in France in 1354.

Almost 40 years later, after being displayed publicly, the cloth was denounced by the bishop of Troyes as a "cunningly painted" fake. The Roman Catholic Church has long been of two minds about the shroud (as it has also been about Medjugorje): accepting that it might be inauthentic (leaning that way when radio-carbon dating in 1988 indicated that the linen dated back only to the Middle Ages) yet respectful of what the image says about the suffering and sacrifice of Jesus. In modern times, in 1958, Pope Pius XII said the image on the shroud was absolutely acceptable when exercising devotion to the Holy Face of Jesus. When the shroud was displayed to the public for eight weeks in the spring of 1998, Pope John Paul II, who certainly had a mystical bent, traveled from Rome to Turin to venerate the relic. Two years later his chief authority in doctrinal affairs, Cardinal Joseph Ratzinger, wrote that the Shroud of Turin is "a truly mysterious image, which no human artistry was capable of producing. In some inexplicable way, it appeared imprinted upon cloth and believed to show the true face of Christ, the crucified and risen Lord." In 2010, Ratzinger, now as Pope Benedict XVI, joined the horde of pilgrims in Turin when the shroud was again displayed. An "extraordinary Icon," he proclaimed it: the "Icon of Holy Saturday . . . corresponding in every way to what the Gospels tell us of Jesus . . . an Icon written in blood, the blood of a man who was scourged, crowned with thorns, crucified and whose right side was pierced . . . [In the shroud] we see, as in a mirror, our suffering in the suffering of Christ." Pope Francis, in his early days on Saint Peter's throne, also used the word *icon* in reference to the shroud.

The dissent was probably most succinctly put by the famous religious leader John Calvin in the 16th century, who pointed out in his *Treatise on Relics* that this stunning and stunningly important thing had been lost for more than 1,300 years. "How is it possible that those sacred historians, who carefully related all the miracles that took place at Christ's death, should have omitted to mention one so remarkable as the likeness of the body of our Lord remaining on its wrapping sheet?" He was referring to all of the Gospel writers (those of the Synoptic Gospels did have Jesus being wrapped in a cloth), then singled out John's account of a cloth over the face: "Either St. John is a liar" or proponents of the shroud are "convicted of falsehood and deceit." The Catholic response to Calvin has long been: *Hmmpfh.* Calvinist. *Protestant.*

So the game was on—a long, long time ago.

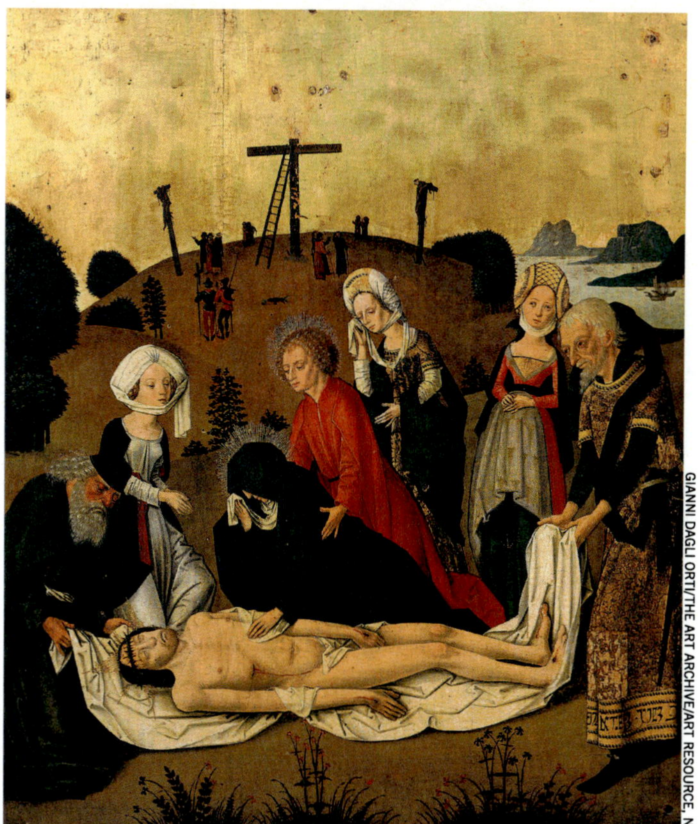

GIANNI DAGLI ORTI/THE ART ARCHIVE/ART RESOURCE, NY

ALFREDO DAGLI ORTI/THE ART ARCHIVE/ART RESOURCE, NY

ROGER VIOLLET COLLECTION/GETTY

© 1978 BARRIE M. SCHWORTZ COLLECTION/STERA, INC. (2)

© 1978 MARK EVANS COLLECTION/STERA, INC.

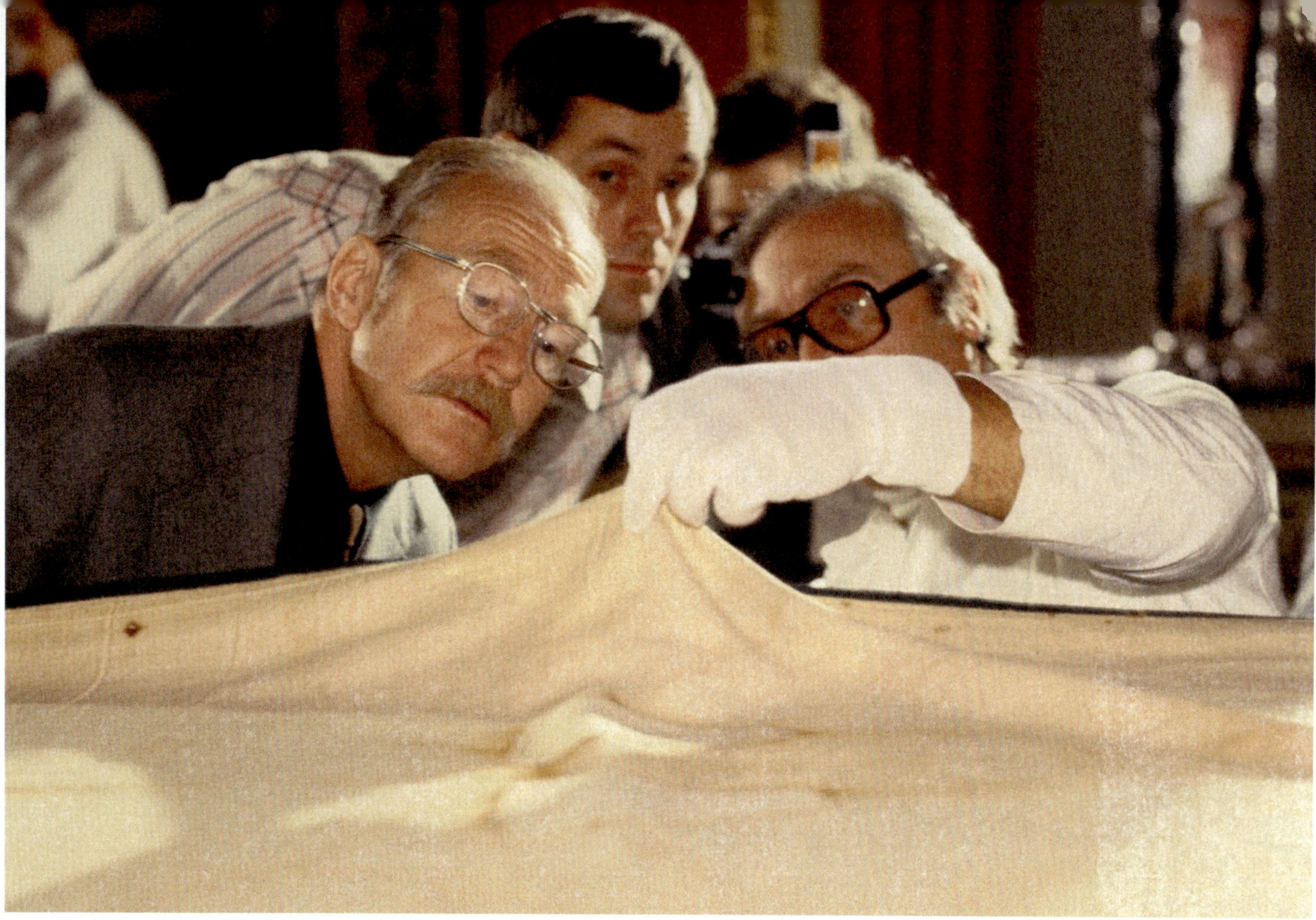

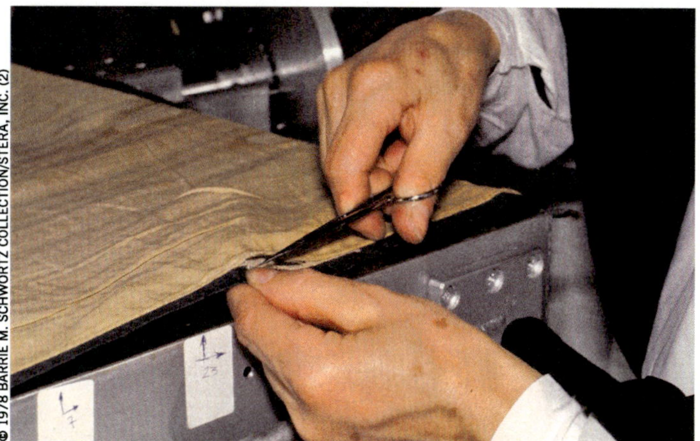

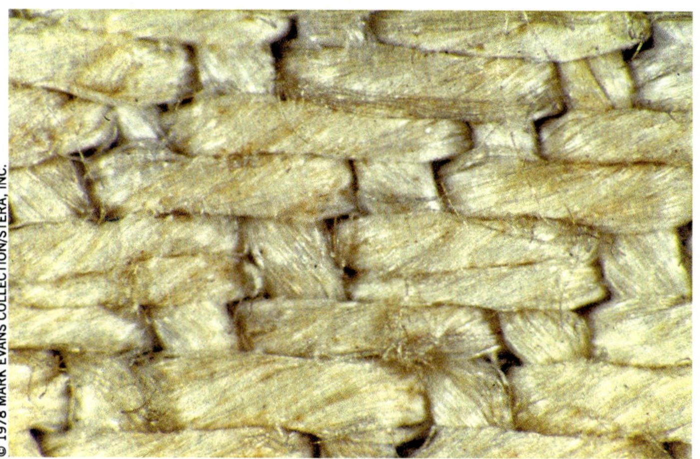

## CALL IN THE SCIENTISTS

The Church and natural science have never been tight; beyond the overarching question of the essence of Creation and whether the theory of evolution can square with biblical teaching, all we need as specific evidence is that the devout Galileo Galilei, father of modern physics, was tried and sentenced by the Inquisition in 1633 for "vehement suspicion of heresy."

Nothing miraculous in Catholic history, however, has so obviously presented itself for scientific analysis as the Shroud of Turin. Even in the Middle Ages, people tried to figure out if the bloodstains had been painted on. Once a photographic negative rendered the image of the body so much more detailed—and startling—further inquiry was demanded.

History was presented to the early analysts: You'll see burn holes, scorch marks and water damage from 1532 when a fire broke out at a chapel in Chambéry, France, where the shroud had been stored. Ignore all that. Tell us: Is this Jesus?

In the early 1900s, French zoologist Yves Delage (opposite) tried to resolve the issue. Above: In 1978, scientists (from left) Ray Rogers, John Jackson and Giovanni Riggi were allowed to experiment as well. Left, top shows a sample being taken and below it, a photomicrograph of the linen during the 1978 analysis. The study by Rogers and his colleagues concluded that the shroud was *not* "the product of an artist," but the men could not determine how the image was created. A decade later, radiocarbon dating suggested the shroud was a fake, but more recent examinations have implied a first-century origin: Jesus's time.

We are all still trying to find an answer.

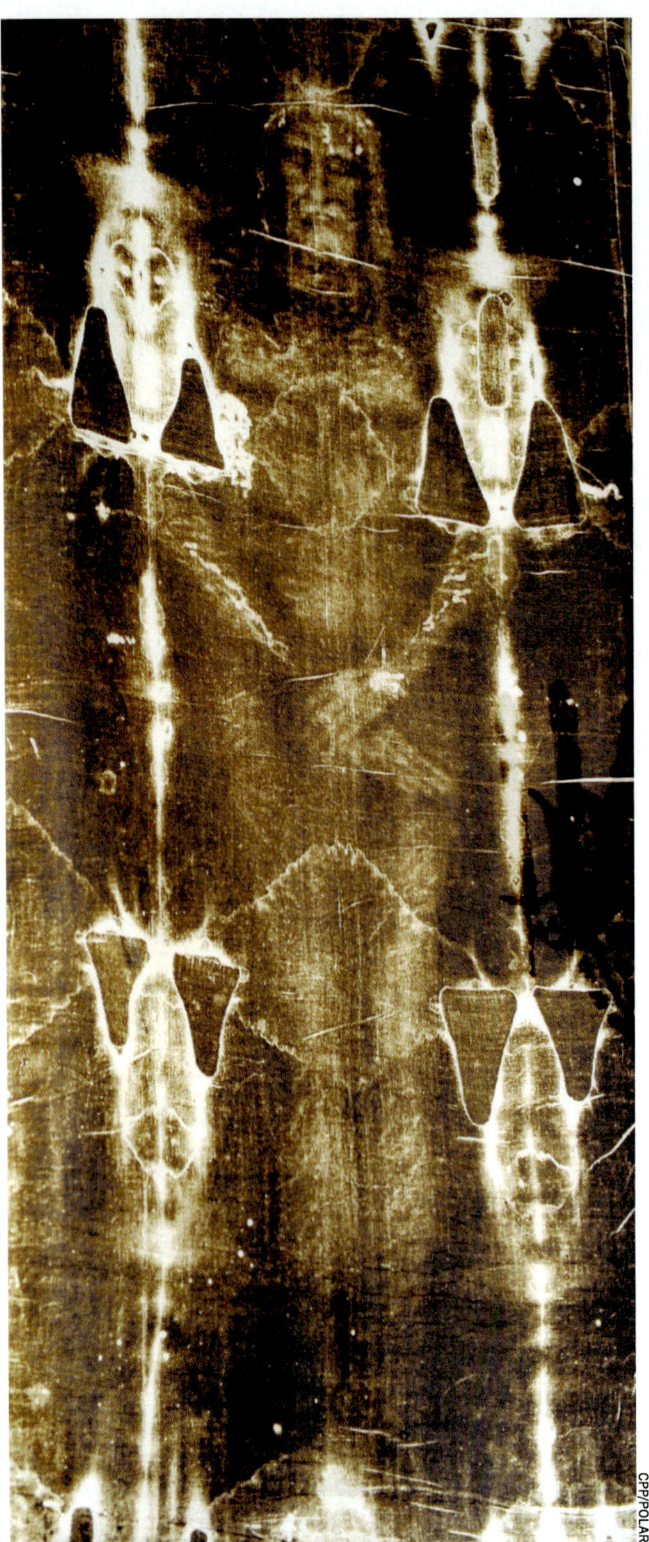

CPP/POLARIS

## A SHOCKING PHOTOGRAPHIC IMAGE

Through the years, the shroud has been put on public display fewer than two dozen times. One important exposition came in 1898, when Italy was celebrating the 50th anniversary of its constitution. In honor of the moment, the shroud was put on display and allowed to be photographed for the first time, by amateur photographer Secondo Pia. It was Pia's observation of a negative image on the reverse photographic plate that so shocked him—and that was so revelatory to others. You can see from the image at left of a shroud reproduction that the details of the subject's image—the dead Christ's or whomever's—are hard to distinguish by just looking at the cloth itself. Above: On April 10, 2010, bishops attend the solemn Exposition of the Holy Shroud in advance of Pope Benedict XVI's arrival.

Whenever the shroud is brought forth from the casket, pilgrims, from paupers to the pontiff, flock to Turin; at that most recent 2010 extravaganza, for example, an estimated 2 million

VALERIO PENNICINO/GETTY

came. The reason is elemental: This is an extraordinary (to use Rome's carefully chosen word) icon to view and contemplate.

It's not merely a painting. It is so much more substantial than one of the hundreds of slivers that supposedly were part of the True Cross. This cloth may have touched Jesus. His Resurrection may have occurred—Him alone in the tomb—while He was sheathed in this. When one sits and gazes upon the shroud, one contemplates Christ, surely, but also pain, human suffering, transcendence—and whether God perhaps wrought one more miracle and somehow left us this artifact to spur such meditations.

Smarter (or at least more technologically advanced) scientists will follow ours. Some of them will no doubt tackle the shroud anew. If a team in the future casts doubt on the shroud's authenticity, then the faithful will say: Wait a decade. Things may change.

It's ironic, in a way. We have worked so hard to find the answer to this. And it is not at all clear that we want or need one.

# Modern

## Miracles

*The Shroud of Turin is a perfect transition: an ancient relic enduring into the modern age, and in the modern age being subjected to new scrutiny. Yet when the shroud is put on display in this modern age, 2 million people line up. As Americans, to return to an even more emphatic statistic, at least 80 percent of us believe in miracles today. Other parts of the world are equally (or even more deeply) believing. People have talked about Moses's time as an Age of Miracles. Or Jesus's, or the Middle Ages. They all were, and we still live in an age of miracles.*

JONAS BENDIKSEN/MAGNUM

In Transnistria, a breakaway republic with scant recognition, existing in the border region between Moldova and Ukraine, religion is important and unifying. Ninety-one percent of the population is Eastern Orthodox and another 4 percent is Roman Catholic. The government says it supports scores of religions, but it has been criticized for persecuting certain Christian denominations—which leads one to wonder about the treatment of non-Christians. So it has the ancient problems and also the time-held beliefs: Baptism in the river will cleanse and initiate.

BOB JACKSON/THE DENVER POST/GETTY

NATIONAL PORTRAIT GALLERY/SMITHSONIAN INSTITUTION, USA/BRIDGEMAN IMAGES

LES STONE/POLARIS

## THE PREFERRED NAME: LATTER-DAY SAINTS

Mormonism is certainly having a moment, though perhaps not the one it would have wished. It has become a favorite topic of the satirists Trey Parker and Matt Stone—its very founding has been a subject on their television show *South Park,* and the entirety of Mormonism has been the subject of Parker and Stone's hit Broadway musical, *The Book of Mormon.*

Poking fun at organized religion is nothing new; Mark Twain did it all the time. One way to look at this (the silver lining): You've arrived.

And when did Mormonism arrive? Well, *Mormon* refers to the religion's adherence to the Book of Mormon, which is, with the Bible, one of the faith's seminal texts and the one that describes the group's particular heritage. In upstate New York in 1823, Joseph Smith (in a 19th-century portrait, opposite page, far left) began to experience visions. An angel told him to find a buried book written on golden plates, which he did, and to read therein the story of an ancient religion. This narrative Smith would publish as the Book of Mormon (Mormon being the long-ago prophet who first wrote the story). Smith's Church of Christ spread mildly westward but did not immediately prosper. Ohio did prove receptive, and soon that was a headquarters. In Missouri, Smith planned to build Zion, a New Jerusalem, and after initial resistance found a home in Lake County. Smith's personal legend grew—he was said to have been visited by Jesus when he, Smith, was 14, and the image of Christ in America (above) became central to the religion—but there were difficulties. A Mormon bank failure led to a further uprooting of the community, and in 1838 the so-called Mormon War with Missouri natives—the governor declaring "Mormons must be treated as enemies"—forced Smith's people to the western fringe of the state.

If we now accept that the Mormon promised land was the West, Smith, like Moses, never reached it. He was killed by a mob in 1844. Brigham Young took the flock, with their unique views and ideas (including polygamy, which would over the years lead to conflicts with local, state and federal authorities), to Utah, and they are well established there. The Mormons are dedicated to service, have a stunning temple in Salt Lake City, sponsor one of the world's foremost choirs—a truly heavenly sound—and are a thoroughly American religion. Ever since they moved west (opposite, a three-month re-creation of the journey on the 150th anniversary in 1997), they have been great.

## SPREADING THE WORD, AMERICAN STYLE

H*allelujah* is a transliteration of a Hebrew word—actually a conjoining of two words—but it seems so very American, having been raised so often in shout or song by all sorts of evangelicals, soothsayers and, yes, snake-oil salesmen. One of the greatest American religious figures in history is Billy Graham, whom we will see on the following pages, and he was certainly a firebrand, if not strictly fire-and-brimstone, when he was young. But then there have been such as Aimee Semple McPherson, presiding on the opposite page, top, at the June 14, 1943, edition of her regular Sunday night service, which was broadcast on the radio from the Angelus Temple in Los Angeles. Sister Aimee was posited as a faith healer but was at least as much a charlatan, which did nothing to diminish her great fame.

In the photograph opposite, bottom, is the evangelist Father Divine, smiling as he leads a parade of nearly 2,000 followers in New York City on August 20, 1936. He claimed to be God, no less.

Above: Members of the Pentecostal Church of God, a faith-healing sect, surround a woman who has "got the Spirit" as a man holds a snake above her head in Evarts, Kentucky, on August 22, 1944. Although a Kentucky statute forbade the handling of snakes in connection with religious services, this sect was happy to pose for a picture. Some folks have given miracles a bad name.

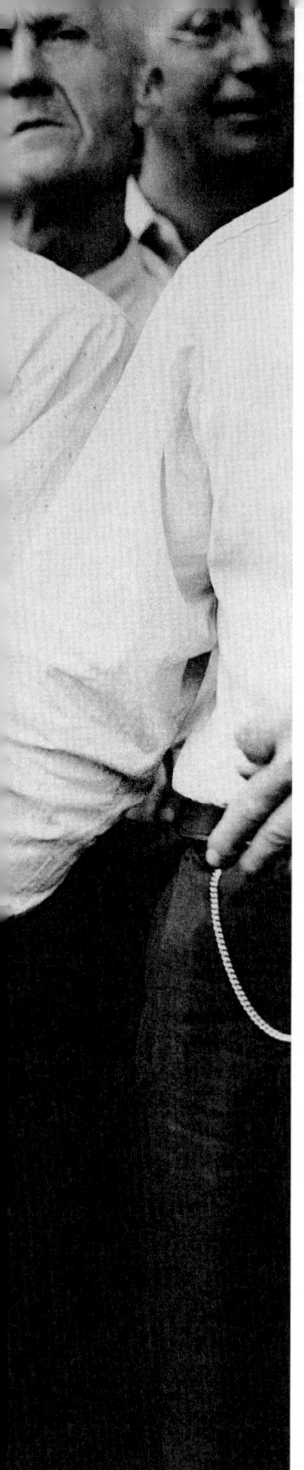

AP (2)

DAILY NEWS/AP

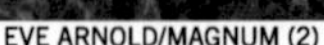

EVE ARNOLD/MAGNUM (2)

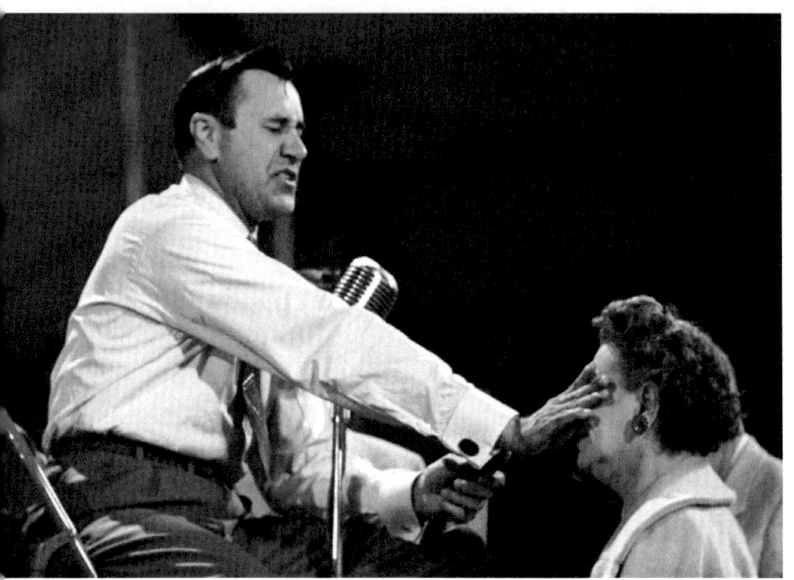

## THE EVANGELIST'S ZEAL

Today there are megachurches. We have survived the period of scandal (Jimmy Swaggart, the Bakkers) and appear to have arrived at a period of telegenic pastors who seem to truly care. Back in the day, when American evangelists were transitioning from revival meetings to indoor arenas, there were certain sons and daughters of Billy Sunday who, by preaching the Word in riveting ways, reached multitudes of people. (Always remember: Jesus, in a time of Zealots, was a Zealot.)

At left, Oral Roberts tries to heal a blind woman by the laying on of hands in 1956. He was one of the first to make the successful transition to both radio and television, and today there is a great university founded by him. On the opposite page is Billy Graham, America's Preacher, delivering a sermon at New York City's Madison Square Garden in 1957. He has been one of the rare American religious personalities to become a global figure, and has counseled a stream of U.S. Presidents, African tribal leaders and even Catholic clerics in Rome. Above: That old-time religion at an Oral Roberts tent-meeting healing session in Minnesota in 1960.

CORNELL CAPA/INTERNATIONAL CENTER OF PHOTOGRAPHY/MAGNUM

JIM LO SCALZO/EPA/CORBIS

PAUL WEINBERG/ANZENBERGER/REDUX

## SACRAMENTAL

Many of the miracles discussed in this book have been either grandiose and historic (waters parting, the dead being raised) or more recent and based on faith (visions, epiphanies). Are there entirely invisible miracles, as some of us believe? What, precisely, is a "miracle"?

In the Bible there are the supernatural occurrences (the Greek definition of the word *miracle: dunamis*), the signs (*semeion*) and wonders (*thaumasias*). There are also works (*ergon*) and fantastic deeds (*kratos*).

But in the faith—in the religion, whatever religion it might be—things are said to sometimes occur, unseen if not unfelt, by agreement.

On this page are two baptisms. Outdoor baptisms, which of course dated to the time of Jesus and even earlier, were a routine ritual in the United States among 18th-century African slaves. They had begun to dwindle in the 1950s with the rise of indoor baptismal pools in churches. But recently, an increasing number of Baptist churches have started to take to the nearby rivers, lakes, oceans and even fire hoses. "It's a rediscovery," said Gregory Hughes, pastor of True Life Ministries, at the annual ocean

KAREL NAVARRO/AP

baptism in St. Simon's Island, Georgia, seen opposite, at top. "It's a way to embrace tradition while renewing our spirit."

The renewal of the spirit was fine that day, and also for the man in the picture on the opposite page, at bottom. He is at a Zionist church ritual in Durban, South Africa, in April 1999. He, like the Georgians, is an adult. The "renewal of the spirit" is an amorphous benefit that we, if we are expectant, are happy to welcome. But what happens when an infant is baptized? There is no volition. What do we think is transpiring?

On a daily basis in the Roman Catholic Church there is a worldwide miracle. At Holy Communion, the Host doesn't *represent* Christ; it *is* Christ: It becomes His body. And then we receive it. Most Protestants don't agree that there is this metaphysical transformation, and others won't even hear of it, but Catholics are asked to accept: This is Christ. In the photograph above, a young girl, having been educated in what is about to happen, holds a candle during her First Communion at Nuestra Señora de la Merced church in Lima, Peru. The day is Thursday, December 8, 2011—the Feast of the Immaculate Conception, a day on which thousands of children in Peru are making their First Communion. This is perfect. A miracle is about to occur, at a moment when she is thinking of Mary, the mother of miracles.

LYNN JOHNSON/NATIONAL GEOGRAPHIC CREATIVE

JEAN CLAUDE MOSCHETTI/REA/REDUX

## THE FIRE OF GOD'S LOVE

Here we have the very old and very new. Opposite is the annual Holy Fire (or Holy Light) ceremony, in which Orthodox Christians gather in the Church of the Holy Sepulchre in Jerusalem on Great Saturday, the eve of the Orthodox Easter, to witness or at least acknowledge the possibility of a miracle. Through the centuries, many Orthodox have sworn that blue light emanates from the stone that covers the place where, supposedly, Jesus was laid to rest. As told by a 20th-century witness, Patriarch Diodoros of Jerusalem: "I enter the tomb and kneel in holy fear in front of the place where Christ lay after His death and where He rose again from the dead . . . I find my way through the darkness towards the inner chamber in which I fall on my knees. Here I say certain prayers that have been handed down to us through the centuries and, having said them, I wait. Sometimes I may wait a few minutes, but normally the miracle happens immediately after I have said the prayers. From the core of the very stone on which Jesus lay an indefinable light pours forth. It usually has a blue tint, but the color may change and take many different hues. It cannot be described in human terms. The light rises out of the stone as mist may rise out of a lake—it almost looks as if the stone is covered by a moist cloud, but it is light. This light each year behaves differently. Sometimes it covers just the stone, while other times it gives light to the whole sepulchre, so that people who stand outside the tomb and look into it will see it filled with light. The light does not burn—I have never had my beard burnt in all the sixteen years I have been Patriarch in Jerusalem and have received the Holy Fire . . . At a certain point the light rises and forms a column in which the fire is of a different nature, so that I am able to light my candles from it. When I thus have received the flame on my candles, I go out and give the fire first to the Armenian Patriarch and then to the Coptic. Hereafter I give the flame to all people present in the Church."

A vivid scene, as is the one in Ondo, Nigeria, above—at one of Reinhard Bonnke's "Fire Conferences," which have been staged in many different countries throughout the world and are evangelistic in the way of many American Christian movements. Bonnke, who is German, says he has preached to more than 120 million people in the past 22 years. Perhaps none other of his megameetings produced such a spiritual picture as this intimate one in Nigeria.

79
ST. MATTHEW 22
37. Jesus said unto him. Thou shall love the Lord thy God with all thy heart and all thy soul, And with all thy mind.
38. This is the First Great Commandment.
ST. MATTHEW 22
39. And the Second is Like unto it. Thou shalt Love thy Neighbor as Thy-self.
40. On these Two Commandments Hang all the Law and the Prophets.
PLACE OF PRAYER FOR ALL NATIONS
O PRAISE THE LORD ALL YE NATIONS: PRAISE HIM ALL YE HIS PEOPLE. FOR HIS MERCIFUL KINDNESS IS GREAT TOWARD US: AND THE TRUTH OF THE LORD ENDURETH FOR EVER. PRAISE YE THE LORD. PSALMS 117 " 118-24 " 33-4
COME! SEE AND HEAR! ALL WELCOME
REJOICE AND BE EXCEEDING GLAD: FOR GREAT IS YOUR REWARD IN HEAVEN: FOR SO PERSECUTED THEY THE PROPHETS WHICH WERE BEFORE YOU. ST. MATTHEW 5-12 II CHRONICLES 36-16
MAJOR PROPHETS
MINOR PROPHETS
TIME Every Sunday 2-2:30 P.M. ON STATION W.H.B.I.
COME! SEE & HEAR OUR SUNDAY RADIO BROADCASTS
ELDER E. BIVINS PASTOR. All Welcome
77

# Carl Mydans and the Pentecostals

*The original title of the 11-page feature that ran in* LIFE *in 1958 was "The Third Force in Christendom," and the subheadline read "Gospel-singing, Doomsday-preaching Sects Emerge as a Mighty Movement in World Religion." As strains of Protestantism embraced a new transcendence,* LIFE *was on the story.*

IN THE PREFACE OF OUR BOOK WE TALKED about a duality, even a paradox, in the American Protestant way of religion: a stoicism and rationalism extending back to the Puritans (despite their belief in witches) and Unitarians, and yet a sense of wonder and a longing to let the joy ring out—to let the miracles of God-worship pour forth. Evangelical Protestantism was on the rise in America in the 20th century, particularly Pentecostalism, which had come out of the Holiness movement and, in the early years of the century, had a champion in Charles Parham, a preacher and faith healer. One of his followers, William Joseph Seymour, started the Azusa Street Revival in Los Angeles, which led to a boomlet and then to a big bang. In fact, today there are nearly 500 million Pentecostals worldwide, and the movement is seemingly growing by the hour.

CARL MYDANS/LIFE/THE PICTURE COLLECTION (2)

In 1958, LIFE's editors took note of this ongoing story and sent veteran photographer Carl Mydans out to document it, focusing not just on the Pentecostals but on everything that was going on in this new American religiosity. "The rapture in the faces of the congregation is one manifestation of the fastest-growing Christian movement in the world today," ran the introductory text, "one so dynamic that it stands with Catholicism and historic Protestantism as a third force in Christendom.

"This third force is made up of groups sometimes called 'fringe sects'—those marked, in the extreme, by shouting revivalists, puritanical preachers of doomsday, faith healers, jazzy Gospel singers. Six million Americans, plus 14 million in other lands, are in its ranks as members of about 100 church groups. They range from the emotional Pentecostals to the sober Adventists. Their churches may be converted stores or 2,000-seat edifices . . . The most uninhibited form of worship in the third force can be found in the Pentecostal churches which, split into innumerable sects, have a membership of almost 2 million."

Mydans photographed the famous Oral Roberts—"most noted Pentecostal evangelist, prayed for 54,433 sick last year"—spiritually healing an ill child in Charleston, South Carolina, and hundreds of other Pentecostals in places from the nation's capital to Detroit to Atlanta to Middlesboro, Kentucky, to Malvern, Arkansas, to Klamath Falls, Oregon. The Pentecostal church seen on the opposite page, the Place of Prayer for all Nations, was in New York City. The man at left having his feet washed in emulation of the apostles at the Last Supper was at the Prospect Temple Pentecostal Church in Cincinnati.

*On this page: The children (right) and the adults (below) of the Bethesda Missionary Temple in Detroit; the grown-ups are singing "Thank You Lord for Saving My Soul." From the caption that ran with the 1958 story in* LIFE: *"Though this church is more conservative than Pentecostals, its pastor says, 'You can't take emotion out of religion, but we keep it decent and in order, as Paul advised.'"*

*Opposite page: Elsewhere in Detroit at the Brightmoon Tabernacle, John Van Dyne, 24, is ecstatic in the prayer room. The original caption explains that he "shouts praises to God as a kneeling friend shares his violent supplication. Van Dyne is striving for the 'baptism of the Holy Spirit,' often indicated by 'speaking in tongues,'—a rush of unintelligible, wordlike sounds." From the text: "Though some Pentecostal sects are relatively restrained in their worship, the purpose of all church services is to fill the members with the Holy Spirit. The Bible is presented as a kind of instruction book, its word final. Swingy hymns and passionate preaching stir up the congregation's emotions, and worshipers respond with hand-clapping, arm-waving, loud singing, dancing in the aisles, shouted 'amens.'"*

CARL MYDANS/LIFE/THE PICTURE COLLECTION (3)

CARL MYDANS/LIFE/THE PICTURE COLLECTION (3)

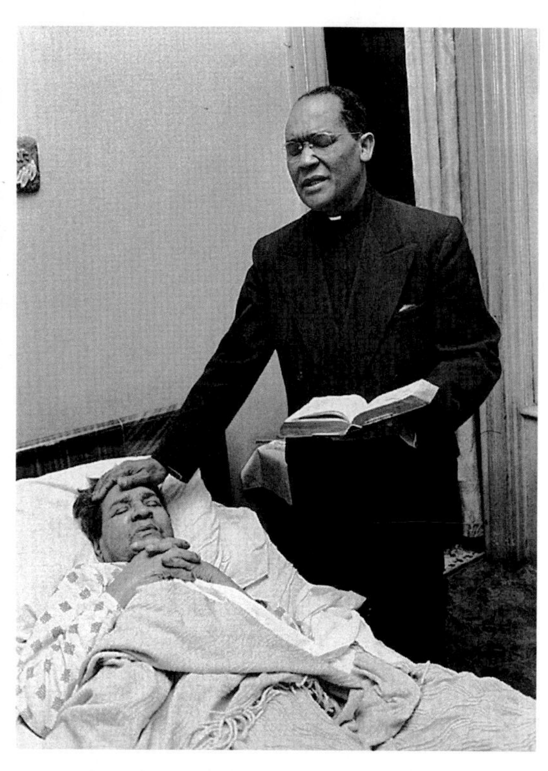

*Opposite: Reverend Dr. Frank Masserano is on guitar at the Bethel Assembly in Memphis, Tennessee. Left: Reverend Frank Negron, pastor of the Spanish Christian Church in Harlem in New York City, prays over the sick. Below: Sidewalk preacher Milton Kean of Glad Tidings Tabernacle tells midtown New Yorkers that the Judgment Day is at hand. "Christ is coming soon! What will the harvest be?"*

*The photographs of Masserano and Kean did not run with the original* LIFE *piece; they are published here for the first time. By contrast, there were several photographs of Negron ministering in various ways and settings, and he was profiled in the text: "The Reverend Frank Negron, 55, who was born in Puerto Rico, is pastor of the Spanish Christian Church in Harlem. He started his preaching career with family prayers while still a factory worker. 'We felt the presence of the Lord,' he recalls, 'and we invited the neighbors to come.' In 1937 he quit his job and was ordained by a group of Pentecostal ministers.*

*"Six nights a week at his 100-member church Pastor Negron holds services which still have the atmosphere of a close-knit family gathering. His daytime hours are taken up with helping his Puerto Rican parishioners, bewildered by their new life. Some need the comfort of prayer, and others need an English-speaking spokesman at the Welfare Department, or the courts, housing agencies, hospitals. 'That's my job,' observes Pastor Negron, '—to help.'"*

# Back to the Garden

FERDINANDO SCIANNA/MAGNUM

WHAT WAS THE ORIGINAL MIRACLE? That question starts a discussion without end. It is not unlike asking, Where was Eden? Some folks say they know the answer to that one and that it was on the Gihon, or the Euphrates, or here—on the Tigris. Is this where God had his heart-to-hearts with Adam and Eve? Is this where it all began?

MANAGING EDITORS Robert Sullivan, Eileen Daspin
DIRECTOR OF PHOTOGRAPHY Christina Lieberman
CREATIVE DIRECTOR Mimi Park
DESIGNER Anne-Michelle Gallero
COPY CHIEFS Barbara Gogan, Parlan McGaw
COPY EDITOR Joel Van Liew
PICTURE EDITOR Rachel Hatch
WRITER-REPORTERS
Hildegard Anderson, Michelle DuPré, Amy Lennard Goehner, Daniel S. Levy
DIRECTOR OF PHOTOGRAPHY EMERITA
Barbara Baker Burrows

**TIME INC. BOOKS**
PUBLISHER Margot Schupf
ASSOCIATE PUBLISHER Allison Devlin
VICE PRESIDENT, FINANCE Terri Lombardi
EXECUTIVE DIRECTOR, MARKETING SERVICES Carol Pittard
EXECUTIVE DIRECTOR, BUSINESS DEVELOPMENT
Suzanne Albert
EXECUTIVE PUBLISHING DIRECTOR Megan Pearlman
FINANCE DIRECTOR Kevin Harrington
ASSOCIATE DIRECTOR OF PUBLICITY Courtney Greenhalgh
ASSISTANT GENERAL COUNSEL Andrew Goldberg
ASSISTANT DIRECTOR, SPECIAL SALES Ilene Schreider
ASSISTANT DIRECTOR, PRODUCTION Susan Chodakiewicz
SENIOR MANAGER, SALES MARKETING Danielle Costa
SENIOR MANAGER, CATEGORY MARKETING Bryan Christian
BRAND MANAGER Katherine Barnet
ASSOCIATE BRAND MANAGER Krystal Venable
ASSOCIATE PREPRESS MANAGER Alex Voznesenskiy

EDITORIAL DIRECTOR Stephen Koepp
ART DIRECTOR Gary Stewart
DIRECTOR OF PHOTOGRAPHY Christina Lieberman
EDITORIAL OPERATIONS DIRECTOR Jamie Roth Major
SENIOR EDITOR Alyssa Smith
ASSISTANT ART DIRECTOR Anne-Michelle Gallero
COPY CHIEF Rina Bander
ASSISTANT MANAGING EDITOR Gina Scauzillo
EDITORIAL ASSISTANT Courtney Mifsud

**TIME INC. PREMEDIA**
Richard K. Prue (Director), Richard Shaffer (Production), Keith Aurelio, Jen Brown, Kevin Hart, Rosalie Khan, Patricia Koh, Marco Lau, Brian Mai, Rudi Papiri, Clara Renauro

SPECIAL THANKS Brad Beatson, Jeremy Biloon, Ian Chin, Rose Cirrincione, Pat Datta, Nicole Fisher, Alison Foster, Joan L. Garrison, Erika Hawxhurst, Kristina Jutzi, Jean Kennedy, Seniqua Koger, Hillary Leary, Melissa Presti, Kate Roncinske, Babette Ross, Dave Rozzelle, Kelsey Smith, Larry Wicker


Published by LIFE BOOKS, an imprint of Time Inc. Books, 225 Liberty Street, New York, NY 10281



Vol. 16, No. 5 • March 18, 2016


We welcome your comments and suggestions about LIFE Books. Please write to us at: LIFE Books, Attention: Book Editors P.O. Box 62310, Tampa, FL 33662-2310

If you would like to order any of our hardcover Collector's Edition books, please call us at 800-327-6388, Monday through Friday, 7 a.m.–9 p.m. Central Time.

Made in the USA
San Bernardino, CA
13 May 2016